Oracle Application Express Forms Converter

A migration guide using the APEX conversion utility

Convert your Oracle Forms applications to Oracle APEX successfully

Douwe Pieter van den Bos

BIRMINGHAM - MUMBAI

Oracle Application Express Forms Converter
A migration guide using the APEX conversion utility

First published: July 2009

Production Reference: 2230709

Published by Packt Publishing Ltd.
32 Lincoln Road
Olton
Birmingham, B27 6PA, UK.

ISBN 978-1-847197-76-4

www.packtpub.com

Cover Image by Parag Kadam (paragvkadam@gmail.com)

Credits

Author
Douwe Pieter van den Bos

Reviewers
David Peake

Dimitri Gielis

Louis-Guillaume Carrier-Bédard

Acquisition Editor
James Lumsden

Development Editor
Siddharth Mangarole

Technical Editors
Aditi Srivastava

Chaitanya Apte

Copy Editor
Sneha Kulkarni

Editorial Team Leader
Abhijeet Deobhakta

Project Team Leader
Lata Basantani

Project Coordinator
Joel Goveya

Proofreader
Laura Booth

Indexer
Hemangini Bari

Production Coordinator
Adline Swetha Jesuthas

Cover Work
Adline Swetha Jesuthas

Foreword

Oracle Forms has been around for a long time. When I started writing computer programs over 20 years ago, I was lucky enough to get to work on an Oracle project where I got to learn all about Oracle Forms 2.3 and Oracle Database 5. Going forward, I worked with most versions of Oracle Forms together with Oracle Designer and some Oracle Reports, and various versions of the Oracle database. I primarily worked on custom development, and so gathered a wealth of Oracle Forms and PL/SQL knowledge.

In 2003, I first learned about a tool called Project Marvel—which is now known as Oracle Application Express, or simply APEX—even before it became an official Oracle product. I was working for Oracle Consulting, and at that time almost every job in Oracle Consulting required Java skills. I was very relieved to find that the skill set for developing APEX applications was primarily PL/SQL. Re-training in APEX is relatively easy as APEX is a declarative framework with numerous wizards for creating screens, which can then be extended using PL/SQL—much the same as the Oracle Forms. There are some fundamental differences in the way the two tools operate. For example, Oracle Forms maintains a continuous connection with the Oracle Database and uses pessimistic locking, whereas APEX only connects to the database when rendering or posting a page and uses optimistic locking.

I joined a project in 2003 for a large law enforcement agency that was actually the primary beta site for APEX. I spent four years on that project, where we were very successful in manually converting several legacy Oracle Forms applications into a suite of APEX applications. That suite now runs the majority of the police departments operations. During my tenure, I trained over 20 Oracle Forms developers in APEX and on an average the developers were productively developing APEX applications within two weeks.

Then in 2007, I transferred from Oracle Consulting to Server Technologies to become the Product Manager for Oracle Application Express. I worked very closely with the APEX Development Team on our Forms Conversion components. Our key objective was to provide a valuable tool that "assists" you in converting Oracle Forms applications. Our intention was never to provide a 100% conversion tool whereby you enter some source files, press a few buttons, and immediately get a production-ready application. Instead, our focus was on automatically converting the components that we can and then providing tracking capabilities through the annotations, which you will learn in detail in this book.

With respect to Oracle Forms, this tool has been utilized extensively to solve business requirements for decades. It is a very robust, high-performance tool that is still being developed and will continue to be supported for years to come. In fact, Oracle Forms 11g was recently released as a part of Oracle Fusion Middleware 11g.

Converting from Oracle Forms to any other technology, including APEX, will require significant time and effort; and should be treated as a project. And that is where this book will prove invaluable—to help you understand not only how the APEX Forms Conversion tool works, but also how to plan and execute your conversion project. This book walks you through the conversion of a sample application and explains the various features. Moreover, it also provides an excellent insight into how you can get the most from using this tool. Douwe Pieter has written a great book that is easy to follow and will definitely help any Oracle Forms developers to better understand what is involved with converting their applications to APEX.

David Peake
Oracle Application Express Product Manager
Server Technologies, Database Tools
Oracle USA Inc.
http://dpeake.blogspot.com

About the Author

Douwe Pieter van den Bos started working as an Oracle Developer using Oracle Designer and Oracle Forms. Soon he discovered the wondrous world of Oracle Application Express and was one of the first people in the Netherlands to be using this tool in real live applications. His first encounters with the development of APEX applications and, later on, his thoughts on web development and project management were written down on his own personal website, `http://ome-b.nl`. This web site became the only Dutch APEX related website and a knowledge base on everything APEX.

Because of his fast experience on Oracle Database development and Oracle Forms, and his 'love' for Oracle Application Express, Douwe Pieter experimented a lot with Oracle Forms to APEX conversion over the last few years, resulting in knowledge about the different challenges this brings. During the Beta tests of APEX 3.2 Douwe Pieter was involved, and he personally ensured that certain requirements weren't overlooked.

Douwe Pieter is a frequent speaker at national and international conferences and has written numerous articles on application development, including APEX-specific application development.

I would like to thank David Peake for giving me more information than I could handle, and Dimitri Gielis and Louis-Guillaume for the brilliant comments and making me see things from a new angle.
I am also grateful to James Lumsden, Siddharth Mangarole, and Joel Goveya for all the work they did for me. I would like to express my gratitude to my mother and sister who thought this was the coolest thing in the world, although they don't have a clue as to what it is about, and also my friends who thought this was just cool enough to celebrate with a few drinks.

About the Reviewers

David Peake joined Oracle in Australia in 1993. He spent the first 13 years in Oracle Consulting, working on various assignments across Australia, New Zealand, and the USA. During this time David concentrated on custom development projects of varying sizes, initially using Oracle Designer and Oracle Forms and later Project Marvel, which when it became an official Oracle product was called HTML DB, before being renamed to Oracle Application Express (APEX). In 2006, he transferred to development within Server Technologies — Database Tools as the Product Manager for Oracle Application Express. David liaises between the APEX development team and the many APEX customers and has presented at numerous conferences around the world. He also contributed on *Beginning Oracle Application Express* by Rick Greenwald (WROX Publishing).

Dimitri Gielis was born in 1978. Together with his family he lives in Leuven, Belgium.

Already at an early age, Dimitri started with computers (Apple II, IBM XT) and he quickly knew he would like to work with computers and especially with databases all his life.

In 2000 Dimitri began his career working as a consultant for Oracle Belgium where he got in touch with almost every Oracle product. His main expertise was in the database area, but at that time he was also exposed to HTML DB which was renamed Oracle Application Express later on. From the very start he liked the Oracle database and APEX so much he never stopped working with it. Dimitri then switched to another company to create an Oracle team and do pre-sales, to later create and manage an Oracle Business Unit.

In 2007 Dimitri co-founded APEX Evangelists (http://www.apex-evangelists.com), together with John Scott. APEX Evangelists is a company which specializes in providing training, development, and consulting specifically for the Oracle Application Express product.

On his blog (`http://dgielis.blogspot.com`) he shares his thoughts and experience about Oracle and especially Oracle Application Express.

Dimitri is a frequent presenter at IOUG Collaborate, ODTUG Kaleidoscope, UKOUG conference, and Oracle Open World. He likes to share his experience and meet other people. He's also the Vice President of the IOUG APEX SIG.

In 2008 Dimitri became an Oracle ACE Director. Oracle ACE Directors are known for their strong credentials as Oracle community enthusiasts and advocates.

You can contact Dimitri at `dimitri.gielis@apex-evangelists.com`.

Louis-Guillaume Carrier-Bédard has been working for the past three years with Oracle Application Express. The APEX community benefits from his blog and tutorials regarding jQuery integration. Developments for the private and public sectors have contributed to build him a solid background. Many projects, from the simple proof of concept to mission critical application, have contributed to Louis-Guillaume's deep knowledge of APEX.

Louis-Guillaume recently joined SIE-Solutions to build systems for SMEs/SMBs. They organize seminars and they launched `www.apexquebec.com`, a web site dedicated to Quebec's Apex community. SIE-Solutions is offering a framework for Oracle APEX.

I would like to say thank you to Clément Carrier, my grandfather. This great man gave me the taste for knowledge and books.

Salut Papi!

Table of Contents

Preface

Oracle Application Express has been around for quite a while now. It has a lot of advantages, such as the possibility to really use the Internet and create fast-performing applications. For the last decade, we developed our applications using another tool, namely Oracle's Forms Developer. Using this development tool for such a long time means we often have a lot of critical applications built in Oracle Forms. But for many people, now is the time to make the transition from Forms to APEX. However, we don't want to develop all our Forms screens again, so Oracle has kindly come up with the Forms Converter for Oracle Application Express in Oracle APEX 3.2.

With the Oracle Forms Conversion tool, we can now generate Oracle Application Express pages from our original Forms (FMB) files. Using this commodity, it is possible to have controllable Forms to APEX Conversion project and in this book we will learn just how to do such projects.

Oracle Forms

Coming from IAF via FastForms and later SQL*Forms, Oracle Forms Developer has been the main GUI development tool on the Oracle Database since version 6. There have been some changes in the product over the years where WebForms was the biggest change, moving from client-server to a web-server environment. It gave the users the possibility to implement a GUI environment over the Web, but the basics stayed the same. The Oracle Forms applications run in a JavaApplet (J2EE) called Jinitior, and have been built using the Oracle Forms Developer and the PL/SQL language.

Moving away from Oracle Forms requires some guts. Most organizations using Forms have large knowledge of the tool and the PL/SQL language, and don't move to a completely different environment in a short period of time. Languages such as Java are difficult to learn and hard to understand for developers not trained in the object-oriented language sets.

And there was APEX.

Oracle Application Express

Oracle Application Express, in short APEX, was a new way of looking at PL/SQL GUI development using only a web browser. Developers could still be using their fast knowledge on PL/SQL and the Oracle Database, and since APEX version 3.2 (released on the February 27, 2009, a memorable day) we were able to convert Oracle Forms applications to APEX easily. This is what this book is all about.

Forms conversion

Using the new possibilities in Oracle Application Express, we will find a new way to create APEX pages from our original Forms and Reports applications. We no longer have to build them from scratch if we want to generate the pages in APEX. Forms Conversion has made it possible to create APEX applications from our Forms and Reports applications in a fast and reliable way. But beware; we still have to do some work to make it all possible. In this book we will point out the steps you will have to take to create your applications using the Forms Conversion tool.

Every Forms and Reports application consists of a few elements, namely Forms modules, Menus, PL/SQL libraries, Object libraries, and Report modules. All these elements will be used in our Forms Conversion project. They will all be translated to their own specific APEX components during the conversion.

In the following diagram provided to us from Oracle, you can clearly see which steps need to be taken, and in which order, to create and execute a Forms Conversion project. As we can see, the main part of the project will be done in the **Oracle Application Express Forms Converter**.

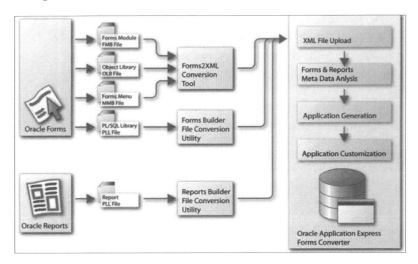

With our Forms Conversion project, we will have to use different tools to create our APEX application. Of course, we will have to use APEX as it contains the most important piece of tooling we have got, the APEX Forms Conversion tool. But besides that we will have to use Forms and Reports Builder, the File Conversion Utilities, and the Forms2XML Conversion Tool.

In this book we will generally learn how to create suitable XML files, but most work in our Forms Conversion project will be done in APEX.

Generate Application Express applications

In order to generate an APEX application, we will have to do some steps. First, we will have to create our XML files from the different Forms components. After that, we shall create our Conversion project in Oracle Application Express.

The project page is the point where we will be really working on our Forms Conversion. Because of the possibilities it gives us, we will learn how to analyze and adjust our Forms components in order to generate an APEX application.

The following screenshot shows the project home page in the APEX Forms Converter. This page is used to control our project and it shows our progress in the project.

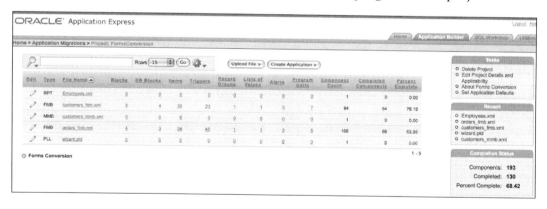

Using the project home page in the Forms Conversion part of APEX, we can easily scan our application components and see how we are progressing. This is the place where we do our metadata analysis of the XML files we uploaded and the ones our project consists of. We can see all the elements of our Forms Conversion project, so we have a point where we can control everything we need to do in our project in the project home page.

Even after generating our APEX application, we will have some other things to do. Because of the large differences between APEX and Forms, we will need to adjust some things such as the logic and the User Interface defaults. We will see how the APEX application we generated responds to users, and how we need to make some adjustments in order to create a user-friendly and stable application.

Possibilities and benefits

Web 2.0 has taken a leap in the last few years; interactive user interfaces and the possibilities of tying applications together are the cornerstones of Oracle Application Express. Modern Internet applications offer users the possibility to create and adjust their own information just as a desktop application would, but with the advantages of accessing the applications over the Internet. APEX offers a lot of these Web 2.0 components out of the box, such as interactive reporting and flash charts. With interactive reporting, the users can define their own reporting, meaning they have control over the filters, break points, and calculations done in these reports.

Both Forms and APEX are completely SQL and PL/SQL based, so the transition from Forms to APEX should be easy to learn. Both tools are declarative, wizard-driven, rapid development tools. With the use of the Forms Conversion tool, it will be possible to speed up the transition to APEX within your organization. The tool uses our knowledge of the Forms applications we convert to let us make the best choices possible.

Oracle Application Express and, therefore, the Forms Conversion Tool is a no-cost option on the Oracle Database. Because of this and the fact that we no longer need an Application Server, APEX is the choice to make if you want to convert your Forms and Report applications to a web environment.

The Forms Conversion in Oracle Application Express offers us numerous possibilities when generating APEX pages from our original Forms, Reports, and Menus. These possibilities are extensive and, when wisely used, offer reductions in developer effort. In doing so, our transition from Oracle Forms and Reports to Oracle Application Express should be quicker and easier all round.

Navigating and adjusting logic is possibly the largest possible advantage you can get from the Forms Conversion tool in Application Express. We get information from the metadata (which is in the Forms, Reports, Menus, and Libraries) and have the advantage of knowing about the logic and different components before we begin the conversion.

Comparison

Forms Conversion in Oracle Application Express is not migration but a conversion, as the word literally means. We will generate a different kind of application, namely an Internet application instead of a desktop or a Web Forms application.

Remind yourself that Forms Conversion in Oracle Application Express is not a way to emulate or completely migrate your Forms applications. Your users will get a different kind of application, and hence a different user experience. We will generate an Internet application, which also means that a lot of the functionality we've got in Forms will return in a different way. Forms conversion in Application Express doesn't mean we will have a Forms emulator or a complete replacement for the functionality within the Forms and Reports applications; we will create an interactive web application.

The following screenshot is of the Oracle Forms we will be converting to APEX in this book. In this typical Forms application, 'Customers', runs within a Java applet and, therefore, is used as a true Forms screen. The application that is used here is the Oracle Forms 10g demo application. We will be using it for all the examples in this book. You can download all the necessary files at http://www.oracle.com/technology/products/forms/files/summit10gr2.zip.

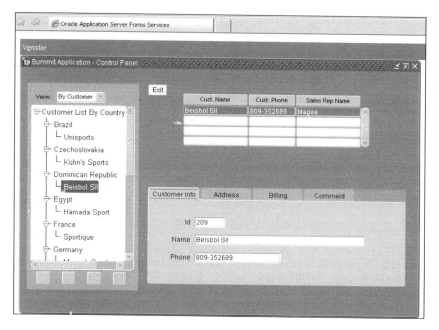

Oracle Forms has a lot of functionality that users appreciate, such as the keyboard shortcuts for a lot of functions (for example, *F11* to enter a query and *Ctrl + F11* to execute it). For people who use these applications, this means they will have a fast-performing and reliable application. All of these native Forms functionalities will not be present in our generated APEX pages. Beware that these functionalities will not be generated during the conversion project. Instead, we will get a fully functional web application built in APEX.

Next, we will see what the application looks like when we have converted it to APEX. In the following screenshot, we see that one master-detail Form **Customers** has been converted to two APEX pages. The following screenshot shows the master data, which is the **Maintain Customer** page:

The following screenshot shows the detailed data, which is the **Customer Details** page:

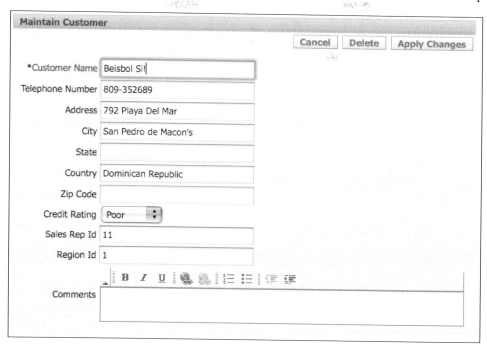

We see here that the pages we create during the Forms Conversion project really are different from the original Forms screens. During a Forms Conversion project, we will have to bear in mind that we will create a different kind of application.

If you're planning a conversion project from Oracle Forms and Reports to Application Express, these differences must be communicated to your users.

The generated APEX pages will have their own advantages. For example, the menus you created in Oracle Forms will be generated as a home page in the new APEX application, complete with icons. In this way will have a new way of navigating through our application. Because APEX uses components that can be described as Web 2.0, the users will get an interactive application in return. And, of course, we can adjust these generated pages according to our taste in the end of the project.

Because the project isn't 'frozen' after the generation of the new APEX pages, we are able to redesign and tweak parts of the application that were not very good to begin with. By taking the Forms Conversion project as a starting point, at the end of the project we can adjust these generated pages according to our taste.

Differences between Forms and APEX

Oracle Forms and APEX have their differences. These differences are not only limited architectural and functional, but are also present in the naming of the elements on which the applications are built. The following table shows how Oracle Forms elements and Oracle APEX elements are related to each other:

Oracle Forms	Oracle APEX
Alerts	Text messages in Shared Components and/or Validations on Application or Page level.
Blocks	Blocks will be generated to Regions in APEX.
Canvases	Are ignored in APEX during conversion.
Editors	HTML Editor.
Lists of Values	The associated record group will be included in the conversion. A List of Values can be developed after generation.
Program Units	Program Units must be implemented after generation as PL/SQL elements.
Triggers	In APEX we don't know the element Trigger. However, there are some things we can implement such as Post-Query Triggers that can be implemented in the Query the page is built on.

As we can see, there are a lot of differences between the two development tools, Forms and APEX. This is not unusual because they both result in different types of applications.

More information

In this book we will provide a lot of information, but because this book is written for developers and analysts who know both Forms and APEX, we will not go into the depths of everything. The following web pages can help you find out more about these topics:

- All the files we use in this book, for example the summit files, can be found at http://www.oracle.com/technology/products/forms/files/summit10gr2.zip.

- You can download and learn more about the Oracle Forms Developer at http://www.oracle.com/technology/products/forms/index.html.

- We will use Oracle SQL Developer in this book, which is a fast, reliable, and free tool for database development by Oracle. More information and downloads can be found at http://www.oracle.com/technology/products/database/sql_developer/index.html.

- The latest stable releases of Oracle APEX and more information about this brilliant tool can be found at http://www.oracle.com/technology/products/database/application_express/index.html or http://apex.oracle.com.

- The most important reference for help with APEX-related (or Oracle related in general) problems is the Oracle Forums. It can be found at http://forums.oracle.com.

- My own web site for all questions related to Forms Conversion is http://www.formsconversion.com. Here you can find more tips and tricks, and where we can discuss matters about Forms Conversion firsthand.

Onwards

In this book we will cover the basics and provide an insight on how to perform a Forms Conversion project using Oracle Application Express. We will go through some critical steps that need to be done to make such a project a success.

Of course, we will need to understand our original Forms and Reports application — how will our conversion project be generated and how does it work?

In Chapter 1 of this book, we learn how we can use our knowledge of Oracle Forms and Reports to our benefit. We will also learn how we can use the powers that are given to us in the Forms Conversion tool to determine various modules and iterations in our project. The original Forms and Reports application is central in this part of the book. This is because, like history, we will need to know our past in order to understand our future.

Chapter 2 shows us what we need to get things ready for our Conversion project. We need to gather all our original Forms, Reports, Menus, and Libraries so that we can generate the APEX project. We will need to get the XML sources by using the tools in the Oracle Developer Suite. Of course, we will learn to understand these newly created sources and what they mean to us. Before we can create our APEX applications using the Forms Conversion tool, it would be nice to design and implement the target database.

In Chapters 3 and 4, we can create ourselves a Forms Conversion Project. Uploading the XML files we just created will create a project for us. We will then learn to add more sources to the project in order to to finalize it (along with the iterations and modules which we defined earlier). The most important part in the Forms Conversion tool in Application Express is the project page and we will learn how to use it, adjust our project, and edit the settings in it.

The project plan is the main part of our Forms Conversion project. The generation is just a small part of the actual project. In what way do we execute our project and can we plan it in order to understand what we have to do? Chapter 4 of this book offers us some ways to judge the components we are about to convert into APEX. We learn some tricks on how to address and timeframe the development. It gives us an insight into what needs to be done and how we will do it.

At this point we will be able to browse the project page in our Forms Conversion project. Chapter 5 will show us how we use the project home page in order to get the logic in our project right. We can make annotations and assign logic to members of the project team who will be responsible for the conversion, and edit the applicability of the different components of our Forms Conversion project. In order to be ready for generation, we need information on our logic so that we can adjust it as needed.

Step-by-step, Chapter 6 will teach us how to generate the new APEX application out of the Forms Conversion project. The settings we applied earlier in our project are used to generate the Application Express application, and we will see how we integrate the menu structure from our Forms application in the new APEX application. Adding pages and choosing the user interface defaults are the additional steps we will take.

After we have generated our APEX application, we will need to review it. We will see what components and pages need further customization and in Chapter 7, we will learn how to do so. With a technical and functional review, we will see how the application works and performs. If we need to adjust logic, user interfaces, or processes in the new application, we will do so.

At the end of every project, we will need to deliver it to our users and production environments. Chapter 8 shows some of the main elements we will have to account for in order to deliver the application correctly. We will learn how to use our project plan in order to test the application and how we need to communicate the differences to our users. To make the new application a success in our production environment, we might integrate it with different modules of our project or with the existing applications. So we will learn what ways there are to do so. At this point we will have succeeded in converting our Forms and Reports applications to Oracle Application Express.

Conventions

In this book, you will find a number of styles of text that distinguish between different kinds of information. Here are some examples of these styles, and an explanation of their meaning.

Code words in text are shown as follows: "We will upload another Forms module, which is a _fmb.xml file."

Any command-line input or output is written as follows:

```
C:>cd C:\summit
```

New terms and **important words** are shown in bold. Words that you see on the screen, in menus or dialog boxes for example, appear in the text like this: "To create a new project, click on the **Create Project** button."

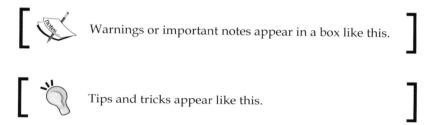

> Warnings or important notes appear in a box like this.

> Tips and tricks appear like this.

Reader feedback

Feedback from our readers is always welcome. Let us know what you think about this book—what you liked or may have disliked. Reader feedback is important for us to develop titles that you really get the most out of.

To send us general feedback, simply send an email to feedback@packtpub.com, and mention the book title via the subject of your message.

If there is a book that you need and would like to see us publish, please send us a note in the **SUGGEST A TITLE** form on www.packtpub.com or email suggest@packtpub.com.

If there is a topic that you have expertise in and you are interested in either writing or contributing to a book on, see our author guide on www.packtpub.com/authors.

Customer support

Now that you are the proud owner of a Packt book, we have a number of things to help you to get the most from your purchase.

Errata

Although we have taken every care to ensure the accuracy of our content, mistakes do happen. If you find a mistake in one of our books—maybe a mistake in the text or the code—we would be grateful if you would report this to us. By doing so, you can save other readers from frustration, and help us to improve subsequent versions of this book. If you find any errata, please report them by visiting http://www.packtpub.com/support, selecting your book, clicking on the **let us know** link, and entering the details of your errata. Once your errata are verified, your submission will be accepted and the errata added to any list of existing errata. Any existing errata can be viewed by selecting your title from http://www.packtpub.com/support.

Piracy

Piracy of copyright material on the Internet is an ongoing problem across all media. At Packt, we take the protection of our copyright and licenses very seriously. If you come across any illegal copies of our works, in any form, on the Internet, please provide us with the location address or website name immediately so that we can pursue a remedy.

Please contact us at copyright@packtpub.com with a link to the suspected pirated material.

We appreciate your help in protecting our authors, and our ability to bring you valuable content.

Questions

You can contact us at questions@packtpub.com if you are having a problem with any aspect of the book, and we will do our best to address it.

Understanding your Project

To understand what we will be doing in our Forms Conversion Project, we will have to know what the application that we are going to convert is all about. What does the application do, both technically and functionally? If we understand why we want to convert the application and how the application works and is built, we will be able to create a more successful conversion project. In this chapter, we will discuss the following:

- What are the reasons for conversion?
- What does the application do?
- How is the application built?
- What are the possible modules and iterations?

Reasons for conversion

Every conversion project has its own reasons as to why it's needed, or wanted. There are lots of different reasons why an IT department or the users want a conversion project from the Forms applications to **Application Exchange (APEX)**. If we divide these reasons into functional and technical categories, we will be able to pinpoint how the converted application must work. In other words, if we understand the benefits the organization gets from moving from Forms and Reports to APEX, the choices we have to make in our project will be a lot easier.

Functional reasons

There are a lot of questions we will ask our users and functional departments in order to get the picture of the great 'Why'. To fully understand why we do this conversion project, we will have to investigate the problems, difficulties, or unwanted restrictions that users are having with the current application. If we want to create a good project plan, we will have to know which of these questions must be answered.

These underlying reasons for conversion must be seen as new functional requirements in the new application. In this way, we will be able to understand how the new application must function after conversion, how it has to look, and what it's supposed to do.

There are a lot of different questions that must be answered before we start our project. The following are a few examples of questions that we want to ask. Bear in mind that these questions are indeed examples and every situation will be different.

- Does the converted application need to be accessed from outside the company's network?
- Do the users need the application to be integrated in other web applications or extranet functionalities?
- Will the application be accessible to the users other than those who use it now?
- Is the conversion needed for the functionality that Oracle Forms doesn't offer?
- Do users need to have more control over the information that is displayed in the application?

Some examples of functional requirements might be that the company needs to have some information in the application that is accessible on the Internet. Of course, Oracle Forms can be pushed towards the Web using WebForms, but there's a need for an Oracle Application Server to use this technology. This is a costly solution and we are still working with Oracle Forms. When we use APEX, we no longer need the Oracle Application Server, but rather just an HTTP server.

Another functional reason for conversion is layout, and this might be one of the most important ones. This is because when we use APEX, we can use the graphical layout the company uses for its web site, or intranet site and completely integrate the application.

There are, of course, a lot of reasons why we need to convert the application from Forms to APEX. These might even be requirements that will not be met during the conversion project, but requests for additional functionality that is easily or better build in APEX. In this case, we can use the conversion project as a technical solution to start developing in APEX.

Remember that the examples I stated here are just examples. This means that every organization and, therefore, application will have its own requirements to address.

Technical reasons

Besides functional reasons for conversion, we will also see a lot of technical advantages of a Forms conversion project. Conversion is, in a lot of cases, done with technical reasons. These can be lowering the stress on the application server by using APEX, or lowering the operational costs by getting the application server out of the architecture. But it's also possible that we just want to kick out the jInitiator of the user's PC, or we want an HTML-based application.

Like the functional reasons, there will be a lot of different technical reasons for conversion to APEX. Asking the right question to the right people in your IT department will make you understand why the conversion is done. The following are some example questions that you will have to ask before you begin doing the conversion project:

- Is the conversion done to cut operational costs?
- Do we need to convert the application in order to modernize our environment?
- Is the conversion done because we need completely browser-based applications?
- Do we need the conversion because we want remote development possibilities?

Understanding the functionality

The most important task in the Forms conversion is that we create an application that the user wants, and will be able to understand and use. In order to make the project a success, we will want to know what the application does and why. Maybe, we will be able to find a functional design that was written during the build of the application, but even if we do, we will need to use the application ourselves to know what it does.

Any application is built to serve a business process. In order to understand that process, we must take a deeper look into the application and the process it was built for. The sequence in which we examine the application and the process is completely reliable on the point of view we take. An (technical) engineer would first prefer to take a look inside the application and after that in the process, whereas an analyst will directly dive inside the business process. But because we are converting an application and not redesigning it, the original application will always lead our investigations.

The application

The application that we will be converting has a functionality that is needed by the users of this application. In the original functional design, we will be able to see a lot of these functions. We will have to wonder why the application is originally built as it is. The application was built with a reason and probably has a lot of functionality built in; however, we, as technicians, will not see it firsthand.

The easiest way to understand the application is to ask one of the main users to walk through the application with you. This user can show you how the different screens work and how the flow of the application is set up. The users control and look up information and data in the application. The context of this data is important for our project. If we do not understand what the information is used for, we may make mistakes in creating our conversion project. Every user has his (or her) own interpretation of an application. The best way to fully understand the functionality and, therefore, the business process, is to go through the application with a few different users. Everyone will give a part of the information you are looking for.

In the following screenshot, we see a Forms application that lets the user edit and control the information about the customers of his organization. As we can see, the user has a lot of functionality inside this single forms screen. The user can look up the customers, their address, credit rating, and can also edit this information.

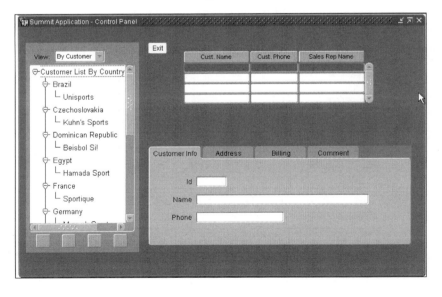

We can look at all the screens in the application. If we do so, we will also have to take a look at the error messages the user gets, the different rights the user has in the screens and, possibly, which user is granted editing and adding rights in the application.

Business process

If you understand the functionality in the screens, it's time to look at the business process that the screens represent. The first thing we will have to look at is the way the user works, what is the user's role in the organization, and why does the user use the application in his or her work? For example, the user probably has some steps to go through if he or she wants to add a customer to the application. Can the user approve the credit rating himself, or is there a different role in the organization for that?

The following Forms screen shows us the **Credit Rating** field in the **Customers** screen. Only users who work for the finance department with the right privileges will be able to edit this information. Because of this role, the business process is covered by multiple departments in the organization and there are multiple roles in the application.

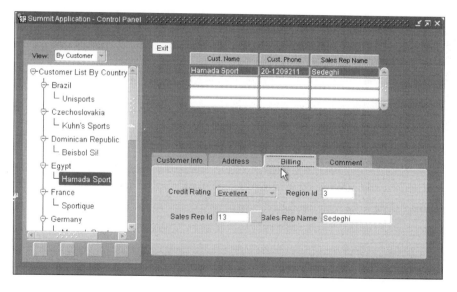

The original application does a lot of things. Following the order of the steps that have to be taken is very important for our conversion project. That's because if we know how the application works, we will know to build certain parts of it such as the screen flow and menu structures.

User interaction

User interaction in the original application is of the essence when we try to understand the application we will have to build. There are some large differences between a Forms application and the one built using Oracle APEX. This means that we need to understand which screens in Forms are most likely to be different. With Oracle Forms, users are used to interacting with their data quite fast. They're used to working with an application that accepts quick entry and even validation is done on the fly. Screens that interact with a user in this way will likely need some JavaScript and AJAX in order to have the same user experience in APEX.

The application does a few different things. Ask the users you interview about the steps he or she would take to do a certain task in the application. For example, if the user wants to add an order for a new customer to the application, he or she first has to create the customer, then the finance department has to approve the credit rating, and then he or she can add the order for this new customer in the order Forms screen. There are certain buttons in the application that take the user to the next step in the business process, and there is a menu that the user uses to get to the next stage of this process.

It's important to understand what the user wants in the application. When we know the required navigation and user experience, we can implement them in APEX.

User roles

We mentioned in the example that the finance department has to approve the credit rating of the customer before the order department can add a new order to this customer. Is the credit rating approved in the same application as the order department? Do the users have the same role in the database, or do we have to take account of some security layers in the application?

The best thing to do in this phase of our project is to make a list of the different business processes and what role the users have in these processes. If we have this list, we can design now and later correctly test our converted application.

Understanding the technicality

Like the functionality of the original application, we are about to convert to APEX and the technical aspects are just as important. As technicians, we will need to know the application and its engine. If we know the sources of this application, we will know what we have to do in our conversion project.

Components

In most Forms applications, we will have more than one Forms screen, and probably even more components of which we will have to take an account. These components are the base of the application and, therefore, the base of our project.

There are a lot of different components in most of the Forms applications. Think about Forms, Reports, Menus, and Libraries. Because we have a lot of different source files, we will need to look at all of these and understand what they do in the application. If we got the different components together, we will better understand how the application is originally built. In this way, we will know the actual size and complexity of the application.

It's always best to make a list of the different components that are in an application we will convert. When we make this list, we will make notes on what components contain which functionality and, approximately, how much work it will be to convert these components. These are the first set of steps to the project plan we will need to have.

Architecture

It's necessary to be familiar with the original architecture of the application. We need to know if the logic that is used in the Forms application is nested in the Oracle Database, or if the logic is all contained in the Forms application itself. Of course, all kinds of flavors are possible here, and so we need to take a look inside the Forms Builder.

If we have an application that contains a lot of code and logic within the PL/SQL libraries on the application server, we will have a lot more trouble converting it than if the Forms application simply calls stored procedures in the database.

In the following example, you see a Forms Builder look on the program units in a Forms application. Here, the procedure calls a Forms trigger that raises a 'Forms Trigger Failure' message. When we perform the Forms conversion, it will be better if we know what the different parts of the application do.

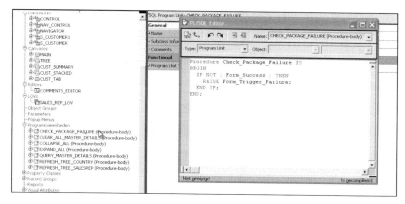

These architectural questions are very important to know before you begin your Forms Conversion project, mainly because a lot of time will be put in the recreation of logic. If the logic is right to begin with, the project will be smaller.

Forms builder

If we look at our different kinds of components—Forms modules, Object Libraries, Forms Menus, PL/SQL Libraries, and Reports Files—we will want to know more about them. How do they work and in what way are they built?

We will have an extensive look at the components in the Forms Builder and the Reports Builder if we have such components in our application. Take a look at the different pieces of information this gives us. We will learn how the screen is built, what triggers and program units there are, and with which properties the original application was built.

In the following screenshot, we can see the canvas of the **Orders** screen in Oracle Forms. As we can see, the application was built on one canvas with a few subcanvases. We got our **MAIN** canvas, which contains four subcanvases: the **TREE** canvas for navigating through the **CUSTOMERS** in the application, the **CUST_SUMMARY** canvas, **CUST_STACKED** canvas, and the **CUSTOMER TAB** canvas.

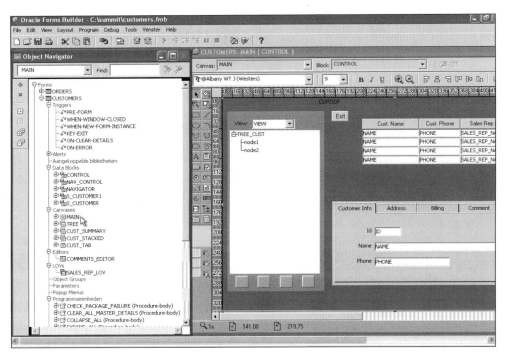

In the following example, we see that multiple are canvases possible in one Forms screen. They react like multiple regions in an APEX application without the **MAIN** canvas. If we know this before, we might be able to convert the application faster and with more insight.

If we look further at our **CUSTOMERS** Forms application, we will see that we are able to know the sources for the data which we use in our application. In the following screenshot, we see the properties of the **S_CUSTOMER** data block in the Forms application **CUSTOMERS**. As we can see, the data block is based on a SQL Query as usual. Surprisingly, the data source comes from the **S_CUSTOMER** table in the database.

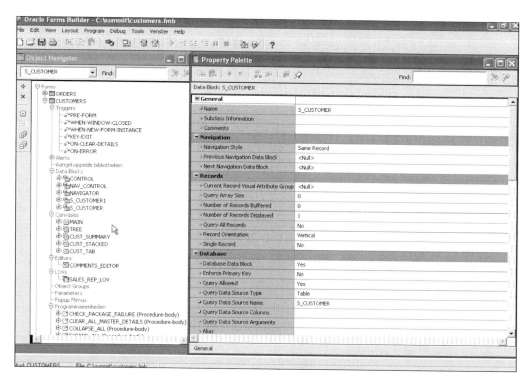

The information we will gather in Forms Developer can also be found the moment we create a Forms conversion project in APEX. In the project page we will see the different data blocks, program units, and other important parts of the Forms application. But at this point, it will be extremely handy to know what we are dealing with.

Modules and iterations

When we create a Forms conversion project in APEX, we will be able to create different applications from one original Forms application. The reason we might want to do this is because we will be able to spread our resources and plan the project a lot better if we cut it into little pieces.

Modular design of the new APEX application will be possible at this point. If we are able to cut the project in different modules and iterations, we have the opportunity to create a reliable project. Every Forms conversion project will know its downsides. Some logic will be difficult to convert and we might need to rewrite it for the conversion project. But it's also possible that our project contains partly non-convertible Forms screens that we will have to build on our own. The parts that are non-convertible will be tracked during the project, so don't let this scare you away.

Remember that non-conversion mostly lies in the way a Forms screen is built. Canvases, Windows, Visual Attributes, and other Forms components will not be in the conversion to APEX because APEX can't use them. When we encounter these elements, we have to adjust the look and feel of APEX itself.

An example of this is that APEX cannot contain more than one tabular form in a page. This means that a basic master detail screen in Oracle Forms will be generated to two APEX pages.

Modules

Modules can be created on functional or technical bases. We can base the functional module on a business process, user role, or even on a logical separate part of the application. If we define the logical or functional modules, we can work with a small team on these modules and even put them in a separate iteration. If we want to cut the project in technical modules, the easiest way is to look at the components on which the application is built. Everything that is interconnected will be placed in one module. In this way, we will have different parts of the application separately. These different parts of the application can be connected to each other at a later stage.

Iterations

When we know the modules, we will create our Forms conversion plan. This is the time to think about the iterations our project will be in. If we have cut the application in functional and/or technical bits, we can combine these into an iteration plan. We will not go into the iterations planning here because we're talking about Forms conversion. But later in this book, we will learn how to combine different modules and iterations together in the technical sense.

Modules and iterations are necessary to keep the project conveniently arranged. The development plan for the project management will be a lot easier with the application divided into little bits. Technically, we will have more applications in the end than what we begin with, but we will combine them together when we deploy the application at the end of our project.

Summary

In this chapter we learned how our application was built. As we will need to make choices in the rest of our project, it helps if we know what the different parts of the application mean. We learned that we had to take the following steps to be ready for conversion:

- We need to understand why we are performing a Forms conversion project. It can be for functional reasons (such as users who need the application outside the office walls) or for technical reasons (such as a need to get rid of the expensive Oracle application server). Of course, it's possible to have a combination.

- To understand the functionality in the original Forms application, we need to take a look at the application itself, the business process it supports, the user interaction, and the roles the users have in the application.

- On the technical side, it can be very helpful if we take a further look at the different components that are in the application, the architecture and how it's built, and the different components in Forms Builder.

- When we know how the application is built, both functionally and technically, we will be able to define different modules in the new application that helps us define iterations for development. During the deployment of the application, we will combine these modules into one application.

2
Preparing your Forms Conversion

Before we start our actual Forms Conversion project, we have to take some steps. We have seen in the previous chapter that we need to understand some things about the application. Now it's time to gather the sources of our application and get our hands dirty.

When we are participating in a Forms Conversion project, it means we take the source files of our application, turn them into XML files, and upload them into the Forms Conversion part of APEX. This chapter describes what we do before uploading the XML files and starting our actual Forms Conversion project.

Get your stuff!

When we talk about source files, it would come in very handy if we got all the right versions of these files. In order to do the Conversion project, we need the same components that are used in the production environment. For these components, we have to get the source files of the components we want to convert. This means we have no use of the runtime files (Oracle Forms runtime files have the FMX extension). In other words, for Forms components we don't need the FMX files, but the FMB source files.

These are a few ground rules we have to take into account:

- We need to make sure that there's no more development on the components we are about to use in our Conversion project. This is because we are now going to *freeze* our sources and new developments won't be taken into the Conversion project at all. So there will be no changes in our project.

- Put all the source files in a safe place. In other words, copy the latest version of your files into a new directory to which only you, and perhaps your teammates, have access.

- If the development team of your organization is using Oracle Designer for the development of its applications, it would be a good idea to generate all the modules from scratch. You would like to use the source on which the runtime files were created only if there are post-generation adjustments to be made in the modules.

We need the following files for our Conversion project:

- Forms Modules: With the FMB extension
- Object Libraries: With the OLB extension
- Forms Menus: With the MMB extension
- PL/SQL Libraries: With the PLL extension
- Report Files: With the RDF, REX, or JSP extensions

When we take these source files, we will be able to create all the necessary XML files that we need for the Forms Conversion project.

Creating XML files

To create XML files, we need three parts of the Oracle Developer Suite. All of these parts come with a normal 10g or 9i installation of the Developer Suite. These three parts are the Forms Builder, the Reports Builder, and the Forms2XML conversion tool. The Forms2XML conversion tool is the most extensive to understand and is used to create XML files from Form modules, Object Libraries, and Forms Menus. So, we will first discuss the possibilities of this tool.

The Forms2XML conversion tool

This tool can be used both from the command line as well as a Java applet. As the command line gives us all the possibilities we need and is as easy as a Java applet, we will only use the command-line possibilities. The `frmf2xml` command comes with some options. The following syntax is used while converting the Forms Modules, the Object Libraries, and the Forms Menus to an XML structure:

```
frmf2xml [option] file [file]
```

In other words, we follow these steps:

1. We first type **frmf2xml**.
2. Alternatively, we give one of the options with it.
3. We tell the command which file we want to convert, and we have the option to address more than one file for the conversion to XML.

We probably want to give the **OVERWRITE=YES** option with our command. This property ensures that the newly created XML file will overwrite the one with the same name in the directory where we are working. If another file with the same name already exists in this directory and we don't give the OVERWRITE option the value YES (the default is NO), the file will not be generated, as we see in the following screenshot:

```
C:\summit>frmf2xml orders.fmb
Oracle Forms 10.1.2 Forms to XML Tool
Copyright(c) 2001, 2005, Oracle.  All rights reserved.

File orders_fmb.xml already exists. Use argument OVERWRITE=YES to replace.

C:\summit>_
```

If there are any images used in modules (Forms or Object Libraries), the Forms2XML tool will refer to the image in the XML file created, and that file will create a TIF file of the image in the directory.

The XML files that are created will be stored in the same directory from which we call the command. It will use the following syntax for the name of the XML file:

- `formname.fmb` will become `formname_fmb.xml`
- `libraryname.olb` will become `libraryname_olb.xml`
- `menuname.mmb` will become `menuname_mmb.xml`

To convert the `.FMB`, `.OLB` and, `.MMB` files to XML, we need to do the following steps in the command prompt:

Forms Modules

The following steps are done in order to convert the .FMB file to XML:

1. We will change the working directory to the directory that has the FMB file. In my example, I have stored all the files in a directory called summit directly under the C drive, like this:

   `C:>cd C:\summit`

2. Now, we can call the frmf2xml command to convert one of our Forms Modules to an XML file. In this example, we convert the orders.fmb module:

   `C:\summit>frmf2xml OVERWRITE=YES orders.fmb`

As we see in the following screenshot, this command creates an XML file called orders_fmb.xml in the working directory:

```
C:\summit>frmf2xml OVERWRITE=YES orders.fmb
Oracle Forms 10.1.2 Forms to XML Tool
Copyright(c) 2001, 2005, Oracle. All rights reserved.

Processing module orders.fmb
XML Module saved as orders_fmb.xml

C:\summit>
```

Object Libraries

To convert the .OLB file to XML, the following steps are needed:

1. We first change the working directory to the directory that the OLB file is in. It's done like this:

   `C:>cd C:\summit`

2. Now we can call the frmf2xml command to convert one of our Object Libraries to an XML file. In this example, we convert the Form_Builder_II.olb library as follows:

   `C:\summit>frmf2xml OVERWRITE=YES Form_Builder_II.olb`

As we see in the following screenshot, the command creates an XML file called
`Form_Builder_II_olb.xml` and two images as `.tif` files in the working directory:

```
C:\summit>frmf2xml OVERWRITE=YES Form_Builder_II.olb
Oracle Forms 10.1.2 Forms to XML Tool
Copyright(c) 2001, 2005, Oracle. All rights reserved.

Processing module Form_Builder_II.olb
Graphics IMAGE3 image saved as FORM_BUILDER_II_REPORT_REPORT_IMAGE3.tif.
Graphics IMAGE3 image saved as FORM_BUILDER_II_PICKLIST1_DEMO_CANVAS_IMAGE3.tif.

XML Module saved as Form_Builder_II_olb.xml
```

Forms Menus

To convert the .MMB file to XML, we follow these steps:

1. We change the working directory to the directory that the .MMB file is in,
   like this:

   ```
   C:>cd C:\summit
   ```

2. Now we can call the `frmf2xml` command to convert one of our Forms Menus
   to an XML file. In this example we convert the `customers.mmb` menu:

   ```
   C:\summit>frmf2xml OVERWRITE=YES customers.mmb
   ```

As we can see in the following screenshot, the command creates an XML file called
`customers_mmb.xml` in the working directory:

```
C:\summit>frmf2xml OVERWRITE=YES customers.mmb
Oracle Forms 10.1.2 Forms to XML Tool
Copyright(c) 2001, 2005, Oracle. All rights reserved.

Processing module customers.mmb
XML Module saved as customers_mmb.xml

C:\summit>
```

Report Files

In our example, we will convert the Customers Report from a RDF file to an XML file.
To do this, we follow the steps given here:

1. We need to open the `Employees.rdf` file with Reports Builder.

2. Open Reports Builder from your **Start** menu. If Reports Builder is opened,
   we need to cancel the wizard that asks us if we want to create a new report.

3. After this we use *Ctrl+O* to open the Report File (or in the menu,
    File | Open) which we want to convert to XML as we see in the
    following screenshot:

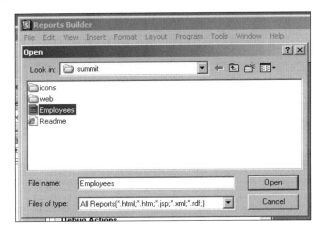

After this we use *Shift+Ctrl+S* (or in the **File | Save As** menu) to save the Report. We choose that we want to save the report as a **Reports XML (*.xml)** file and we click on the **Save** button as shown in the following screenshot:

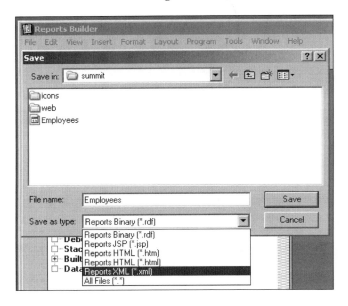

PL/SQL Libraries

To convert PL/SQL Libraries to an XML format, it's easiest to use the `convert` command that comes with the Report Builder. With this command called `rwconverter`, we define the source type, call the source, and define the destination type and the destination. In this way, we have control over the way we need to convert the original `.pll` file to a `.pld` flat file that we can upload into the APEX Forms converter. It is possible to convert the PL/SQL Libraries with the **convert** option in Forms Builder, but, personally, I think this option works better. The `rwconverter` command has a few parameters we give with it to execute. They are given as follows:

- `stype`: This is the type of source file we need to convert. In our situation, this will be a `.pll` file and so the value we need to set is `pllfile`.

- `source`: This is the name of the source file, including the extension. In our case, it is `wizard.pll`.

- `dtype`: This is the file type we want to convert our source file to. In our case, it is a `.pld` file and so the value becomes `pldfile`.

- `dest`: This is the name, including the extension, of the destination file. In our case, it is `wizard.pld`.

In our example, we use the `wizard.pll` file that's in our `summit` files directory. This PL/SQL Library that contains `.pll` files is normally used to create a PL/SQL Library in the Oracle Database. But this time, we will use it to create a `.pld` flat file that we will upload to APEX.

First, we change the directory to work directory which has the original `.pll` file. In our case, we summit the directory directly under the C drive, shown as follows:

```
C:>cd C:\summit
```

After this, we call `rwconverter` in the command prompt as shown here:

```
C:\summit> rwconverter stype=pllfile source=wizard.pll dtype=pldfile
dest=wizard.pld
```

```
C:\Documents and Settings\omeb>cd C:\summit

C:\summit>rwconverter stype=pllfile source=wizard.pll dtype=pldfile dest=wizard.
pld

C:\summit>
```

When you press the *Enter* key, a screen will open that is used to do the conversion. We will see that the types and names of the files are the same as we entered them in the command line. We need to click on the **OK** button to convert the file from .pll to .pld.

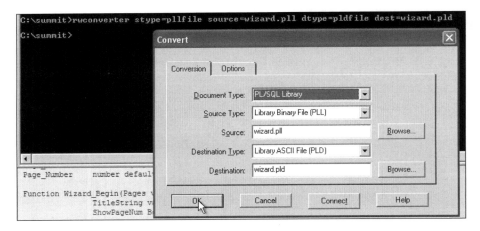

The conversion may take a few seconds, but when the file has been converted we will see a confirmation that the conversion was successful. After this, we can look in the c:\summit directory and we will see that a file wizard.pld is created.

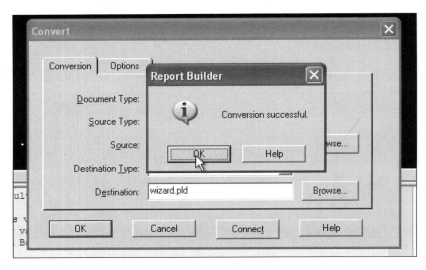

Understanding XML

If we take a look inside the XML files we just created, we will notice a few things. I use SQL Developer of Oracle to look inside the XML files we just created. It's a free tool that we will need for several other tasks during our Conversion project and it does the job. But, of course, you can use a different XML editor to examine the XML files.

When we open SQL Developer, we can open the files we created earlier. The forms, menus, reports, and libraries are now all in XML or flat files. To open the files in SQL Developer, just click on file and then click on **Open** (or use the keyboard shortcuts *Ctrl+O*). Select the file you want to open from the dialog box that's shown in the following screenshot:

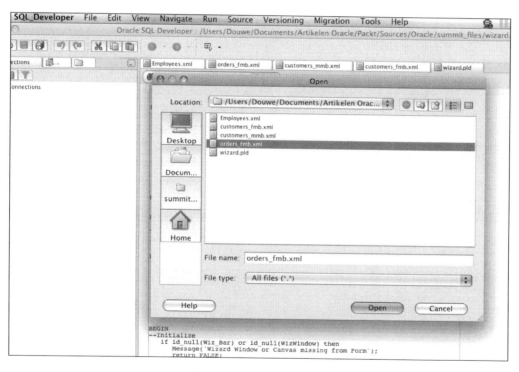

First, we take a look at the Forms Modules in the _fmb.xml files. As you can see, there's a lot of information there. But if we take a further look, we'll see that it's not new information. I will not discuss all of the information that's in the XML files here. For further information about the contents of these files, I recommend reading the *Migration Help* section in Oracle Application Express.

The following screenshot lets us see the contents of the `orders_fmb.xml` file that we created earlier. It shows us the name of the Forms Module (**ORDERS**), the Alerts, the Blocks, and much more. We can see that it's the same information we saw in the previous chapter in the Forms Builder.


```xml
<?xml version = '1.0' encoding = 'UTF-8'?>
<Module version="101020002" xmlns="http://xmlns.oracle.com/Forms">
  <FormModule Name="ORDERS" ConsoleWindow="WIN_ORDER" DirtyInfo="true" MenuModule="m_summit" Title="MODULE2">
    <Coordinate CharacterCellWidth="5" CoordinateSystem="Real" CharacterCellHeight="14" RealUnit="Point" DefaultFo
    <Alert Name="DELETE_ALERT" Button2Label="No" AlertStyle="Caution" Button1Label="Yes"/>
    <Alert Name="QUESTION_ALERT" Button2Label="No" Title="Question" Button1Label="Yes"/>
    <Alert Name="PAYMENT_TYPE_ALERT" AlertMessage="This customer must pay cash!" Button2Label="" AlertStyle="Cauti
    <AttachedLibrary Name="CALENDAR" LibrarySource="File" LibraryLocation="calendar"/>
    <Block Name="Orders" DirtyInfo="true" QueryDataSourceName="S_ORD" ScrollbarWidth="9" DMLDataName="S_ORD" Scrol
      <Item Name="CUSTOMER_NAME" PromptAlign="Start" Height="14" PromptFontName="MS Sans Serif" InsertAllowed="fa
      <Item Name="ID" Height="14" PromptFontName="MS Sans Serif" Width="40" DistanceBetweenRecords="40" PromptDis
      <Item Name="CUSTOMER_ID" Height="14" PromptFontName="MS Sans Serif" Width="66" DistanceBetweenRecords="40"
        <Trigger Name="WHEN-VALIDATE-ITEM" TriggerText="SELECT C.name, C.sales_rep_id, E.last_name&amp;#10;INTO
      </Item>
      <Item Name="DATE_ORDERED" Height="14" PromptFontName="MS Sans Serif" Width="66" DistanceBetweenRecords="40"
        <Trigger Name="KEY-LISTVAL" TriggerText="date_lov.get_date(sysdate,          -- initial date&amp;#10;
      </Item>
      <Item Name="DATE_SHIPPED" Height="14" PromptFontName="MS Sans Serif" Width="66" DistanceBetweenRecords="40"
        <Trigger Name="KEY-LISTVAL" TriggerText="date_lov.get_date(sysdate + 7,          -- initial date&amp;#10;
      </Item>
      <Item Name="SALES_REP_ID" Height="14" PromptFontName="MS Sans Serif" Width="66" DistanceBetweenRecords="40"
      <Item Name="SALES_REP_NAME" Height="14" PromptFontName="MS Sans Serif" InsertAllowed="false" Width="116" Pr
      <Item Name="PAYMENT_TYPE" Height="14" XPosition="121" PromptFontName="MS Sans Serif" PromptFontSpacing="Nor
        <RadioButton Name="CASH_BUTTON" BackColor="FrameColor" AccessKey="S" DirtyInfo="true" Height="14" XPosit
        <RadioButton Name="CREDIT_BUTTON" BackColor="FrameColor" AccessKey="T" DirtyInfo="true" Height="14" XPos
        <Trigger Name="WHEN-RADIO-CHANGED" TriggerText="DECLARE&amp;#10;  N NUMBER;&amp;#10;  v_credit S_CUSTOME
      </Item>
      <Item Name="ORDER_FILLED" Height="14" CheckBoxOtherValues="Not Allowed" PromptFontName="MS Sans Serif" Widt
      <DataSourceColumn Type="Query" DSCType="NUMBER" DSCLength="0" DSCPrecision="7" DSCName="ID" DSCScale="0" DS
      <DataSourceColumn Type="Query" DSCType="NUMBER" DSCLength="0" DSCPrecision="7" DSCName="CUSTOMER_ID" DSCSca
      <DataSourceColumn Type="Query" DSCType="DATE" DSCLength="0" DSCPrecision="0" DSCName="DATE_ORDERED" DSCScal
      <DataSourceColumn Type="Query" DSCType="DATE" DSCLength="0" DSCPrecision="0" DSCName="DATE_SHIPPED" DSCScal
      <DataSourceColumn Type="Query" DSCType="NUMBER" DSCLength="0" DSCPrecision="7" DSCName="SALES_REP_ID" DSCSc
      <DataSourceColumn Type="Query" DSCType="NUMBER" DSCLength="0" DSCPrecision="11" DSCName="TOTAL" DSCScale="2
      <DataSourceColumn Type="Query" DSCType="VARCHAR2" DSCLength="6" DSCPrecision="0" DSCName="PAYMENT_TYPE" DSC
      <DataSourceColumn Type="Query" DSCType="VARCHAR2" DSCLength="1" DSCPrecision="0" DSCName="ORDER_FILLED" DSC
      <Relation Name="S_ORD_S_ITEM" DeleteRecord="Non Isolated" DetailBlock="S_ITEM" AutoQuery="false" PreventMas
      <Trigger Name="KEY-COMMIT" TriggerText="COMMIT_FORM;" DirtyInfo="true" DisplayInKeyboardHelp="true"/>
```


If we take a closer look at one of the blocks in the XML file, for example the **Items** block, we can look for some of the information that APEX uses in the conversion. We can see the names of the **Items** used in this block. We can also look at the queries that are used in this data block and triggers.


```xml
<Block Name="Items" ScrollbarTabPageName="" DirtyInfo="true" ScrollbarWidth="11" DMLDataName="S_ITEM" ScrollbarXP
  <Item Name="ORD_ID" CopyValueFromItem="Orders.ID" Height="14" PromptAlign="Center" XPosition="10" Width="41" R
  <Item Name="ITEM_ID" Height="14" PromptAlign="Center" PromptFontName="MS Sans Serif" Width="20" PromptDisplayS
  <Item Name="PRODUCT_ID" Height="14" PromptAlign="Center" PromptFontName="MS Sans Serif" Width="40" PromptDispl
    <Trigger Name="WHEN-VALIDATE-ITEM" TriggerText="SELECT name, suggested_whlsl_price&amp;#10;INTO :Items.desc
  </Item>
  <Item Name="PRICE" Height="14" PromptAlign="Center" PromptFontName="MS Sans Serif" Width="42" PromptDisplaySty
  <Item Name="QUANTITY" Height="14" PromptAlign="Center" PromptFontName="MS Sans Serif" Width="26" PromptDisplay
  <Item Name="QUANTITY_SHIPPED" Height="14" PromptAlign="Center" PromptFontName="MS Sans Serif" Width="26" Promp
  <Item Name="ITEM_TOTAL" Height="14" PromptAlign="Center" PromptFontName="MS Sans Serif" InsertAllowed="false"
  <Item Name="TOTAL" Height="14" PromptFontName="MS Sans Serif" Width="86" ItemsDisplay="1" MaximumLength="13" P
  <Item Name="DESCRIPTION" PromptAlign="Center" Height="14" PromptFontName="MS Sans Serif" Width="133" MaximumLe
  <Item Name="PRODUCT_IMAGE" Height="113" DirtyInfo="true" XPosition="320" Visible="false" ForegroundColor="blac
  <Item Name="IMAGE_DESCRIPTION" FontSize="800" DirtyInfo="true" Justification="Start" Height="16" XPosition="31
  <DataSourceColumn Type="Query" DSCType="NUMBER" DSCLength="0" DSCPrecision="7" DSCName="ORD_ID" DSCScale="0" D
  <DataSourceColumn Type="Query" DSCType="NUMBER" DSCLength="0" DSCPrecision="7" DSCName="ITEM_ID" DSCScale="0"
  <DataSourceColumn Type="Query" DSCType="NUMBER" DSCLength="0" DSCPrecision="7" DSCName="PRODUCT_ID" DSCScale="
  <DataSourceColumn Type="Query" DSCType="NUMBER" DSCLength="0" DSCPrecision="11" DSCName="PRICE" DSCScale="2" D
  <DataSourceColumn Type="Query" DSCType="NUMBER" DSCLength="0" DSCPrecision="9" DSCName="QUANTITY" DSCScale="0"
  <DataSourceColumn Type="Query" DSCType="NUMBER" DSCLength="0" DSCPrecision="9" DSCName="QUANTITY_SHIPPED" DSCS
  <Relation Name="S_ITEM_S_INVENTORY" DeleteRecord="Isolated" DetailBlock="S_INVENTORY" AutoQuery="true" Prevent
  <Trigger Name="POST-QUERY" TriggerText="SELECT name&amp;#10;INTO :Items.description&amp;#10;FROM S_PRODUCT&amp
  <Trigger Name="WHEN-NEW-RECORD-INSTANCE" TriggerText="DECLARE&amp;#10;  filename VARCHAR2(20);&amp;#10;BEGIN&a
  <Trigger Name="PRE-INSERT" TriggerText="SELECT NVL(MAX(item_id),0) + 1&amp;#10;INTO :Items.item_id&amp;#10;FRO
  <Trigger Name="KEY-DUPREC" TriggerText=":Items.item_id := NULL;&amp;#10;:Items.product_id := NULL;&amp;#10;:It
  <Trigger Name="KEY-DELREC" TriggerText="SET_ALERT_PROPERTY('delete_alert', ALERT_MESSAGE_TEXT, 'Do you want to
  <Trigger Name="ON-POPULATE-DETAILS" TriggerText="--&amp;#10;-- Begin default relation declare section&amp;#10;
  <Trigger Name="KEY-COMMIT" TriggerText="COMMIT_FORM;" DirtyInfo="true" DisplayInKeyboardHelp="true"/>
</Block>
```

Now, let's take a look at one of our Menu Modules, `customers_mmb.xml`. Because we can't convert a menu in a Forms to APEX conversion project, the information in here isn't that interesting. During conversion, we will create some horizontally oriented images that can be used as a menu. But the information held in the **MenuItem Name** tags is interesting to us. You will encounter a few names here that point to a certain form in our application. These names will be used in our conversion project.

```xml
<?xml version = '1.0' encoding = 'UTF-8'?>
<Module version="101020002" xmlns="http://xmlns.oracle.com/Forms">
   <MenuModule Name="CUSTOMERS" DirtyInfo="true" RoleCount="2" MainMenu="MAIN_MENU" StartupCode="begin&amp;#10; dbms_outpu
      <MenuModuleRole Index="2" Value="MANAGERS"/>
      <MenuModuleRole Index="1" Value="CLERKS"/>
      <Menu Name="MAIN_MENU" ParentType="20" DirtyInfo="true" ParentName="TREE_MENU" TearOffMenu="false" ParentModule="CUS
         <MenuItem Name="SAVE" FontSize="1000" DirtyInfo="true" FontName="@Gulim" Comment="this is a test" FontSpacing="Ul
            <MenuItemRole Index="2" Value="MANAGERS"/>
            <MenuItemRole Index="1" Value="CLERKS"/>
         </MenuItem>
         <MenuItem Name="REVERT" DirtyInfo="true" SubclassSubObject="true"/>
         <MenuItem Name="ITEM48" DirtyInfo="true" SubclassSubObject="true"/>
         <MenuItem Name="EXIT" DirtyInfo="true" SubclassSubObject="true"/>
         <MenuItem Name="ITEM59" DirtyInfo="true" SubclassSubObject="true"/>
         <MenuItem Name="ADD" DirtyInfo="true" SubclassSubObject="true"/>
         <MenuItem Name="DELETE" DirtyInfo="true" SubclassSubObject="true"/>
         <MenuItem Name="EDIT" DirtyInfo="true" SubclassSubObject="true"/>
         <MenuItem Name="ITEM60" DirtyInfo="true" SubclassSubObject="true"/>
         <MenuItem Name="SALES_REP" DirtyInfo="true" SubclassSubObject="true"/>
         <MenuItem Name="WINDOW" FontSize="2000" DirtyInfo="true" FontName="@MS PMincho" Comment="this is a comment" Paren
            <MenuItemRole Index="2" Value="MANAGERS"/>
            <MenuItemRole Index="1" Value="CLERKS"/>
         </MenuItem>
         <MenuItem Name="TREE" DirtyInfo="true" IconInMenu="true" VisibleInMenu="true" SubMenuName="TREE_MENU" CommandType
      </Menu>
      <Menu Name="TREE_MENU" DirtyInfo="true">
         <MenuItem Name="SAVE" VisibleInVerticalMenuToolbar="true" DirtyInfo="true" IconInMenu="false" MenuItemCode="commi
         <MenuItem Name="REVERT" DirtyInfo="true" Comment="q" VisibleInHorizontalMenuToolbar="true" Label="Revert" Visible
         <MenuItem Name="ITEM48" VisibleInVerticalMenuToolbar="true" DirtyInfo="true" IconInMenu="false" VisibleInMenu="fa
         <MenuItem Name="EXIT" VisibleInVerticalMenuToolbar="true" DirtyInfo="true" MenuItemCode="do_key('exit_form');" Vi
         <MenuItem Name="ITEM59" VisibleInVerticalMenuToolbar="true" DirtyInfo="true" VisibleInMenu="false" CommandType="N
         <MenuItem Name="ADD" VisibleInVerticalMenuToolbar="true" DirtyInfo="true" IconInMenu="false" MenuItemCode="DECLAR
         <MenuItem Name="DELETE" VisibleInVerticalMenuToolbar="true" DirtyInfo="true" IconInMenu="false" MenuItemCode="dec
         <MenuItem Name="EDIT" VisibleInVerticalMenuToolbar="true" DirtyInfo="true" IconInMenu="false" MenuItemCode="null;
         <MenuItem Name="ITEM60" VisibleInVerticalMenuToolbar="true" DirtyInfo="true" VisibleInMenu="false" CommandType="N
         <MenuItem Name="SALES_REP" VisibleInVerticalMenuToolbar="true" DirtyInfo="true" IconInMenu="true" MenuItemCode="s
      </Menu>
      <ProgramUnit Name="ENABLE_DISABLE_REGULAR_ITEMS" ProgramUnitType="Procedure" ProgramUnitText="procedure enable_disab
      <ProgramUnit Name="ENABLE_DISABLE_QUERY_ITEMS" ProgramUnitType="Procedure" ProgramUnitText="procedure enable_disable
      <ProgramUnit Name="COLLAPSE_ALL" Comment="testing" ProgramUnitType="Procedure" ProgramUnitText="PROCEDURE collapse_a
      <ProgramUnit Name="EXPAND_ALL" ProgramUnitType="Procedure" ProgramUnitText="PROCEDURE expand_all (p_node in ftree.no
      <ProgramUnit Name="REFRESH_TREE_COUNTRY" ProgramUnitType="Procedure" ProgramUnitText="PROCEDURE refresh_tree_country
      <ProgramUnit Name="REFRESH_TREE_SALESREP" ProgramUnitType="Procedure" ProgramUnitText="PROCEDURE refresh_tree_salesr
      <ProgramUnit Name="SALES_REP_INFORMATION" ProgramUnitType="Procedure" ProgramUnitText="PROCEDURE SALES_REP_INFORMATI
   </MenuModule>
</Module>
```

In the XML that we created from our Oracle Reports application, we see a lot of information such as how the report is built, what font is used, some layout information about the building blocks of the reports page, and so on. But none of this information is useful for us. The only thing we need is the query. As we can see in the following screenshot, `Employees.xml` is a fairly big file:

```xml
<?xml version="1.0" encoding="WINDOWS-1252" ?>
<report name="Employees" DTDVersion="9.0.2.0.10">
  <xmlSettings xmlTag="EMPLOYEES" xmlPrologType="text">
  <![CDATA[<?xml version="1.0" encoding="&Encoding"?>]]>
  </xmlSettings>
  <reportHtmlEscapes>
    <afterPageHtmlEscape>
    <![CDATA[<hr size=5 noshade>
]]>
    </afterPageHtmlEscape>
    <beforeFormHtmlEscape>
    <![CDATA[<html dir=&Direction>
<body bgcolor="#ffffff">
<form method=post action="_action_">
<input name="hidden_run_parameters" type=hidden value="_hidden_">
<font color=red><!--error--></font>
<center>
<p><table border=0 cellspacing=0 cellpadding=0>
<tr>
<td><input type=submit></td>
<td width=15>
<td><input type=reset></td>
</tr>
</table>
<p><hr><p>
]]>
    </beforeFormHtmlEscape>
    <pageNavigationHtmlEscape>
    <![CDATA[<!DOCTYPE HTML PUBLIC "-//W3C//DTD HTML 4.01 Transitional//EN">
<html dir=&Direction>
<head>
<meta http-equiv="Content-Type" content="text/html; charset=&Encoding">
<TITLE>Oracle HTML Navigator</TITLE>
<SCRIPT type="text/javascript" LANGUAGE = "JavaScript">

var jump_index = 1      // Jump to this page
var num_pages = &TotalPages     // Total number of pages
var basefilename = "&file_name"    // Base file name
var fileext = "&file_ext"   //File extension

/* jumps to "new_page" */
function new_page(form, new_page)
{
  form.reqpage.value = new_page;
  parent.frames[0].location = basefilename + "_" + new_page + "."+fileext;
}
```

The SQL query we're interested in is set in the **select** tags in this XML file. When we upload the file to the APEX conversion tool, we will use only this information:

```
<select>
    <![CDATA[SELECT ALL S_EMP.ID, S_EMP.LAST_NAME, S_EMP.FIRST_NAME,
S_EMP.START_DATE, S_EMP.USERID, S_EMP.COMMENTS, S_EMP.MANAGER_ID,
S_EMP.TITLE, S_EMP.DEPT_ID, S_EMP.SALARY, S_EMP.COMMISSION_PCT
FROM S_EMP ]]>
    </select>
```

The last things we will discuss in this section are the PL/SQL Libraries. In the
following screenshot, we opened the `wizard.pld` file that we created earlier.
As we can see, it's just a definition of the **Wizard Package** and **Package** body.
To understand this function, it will be useful to look into this code:

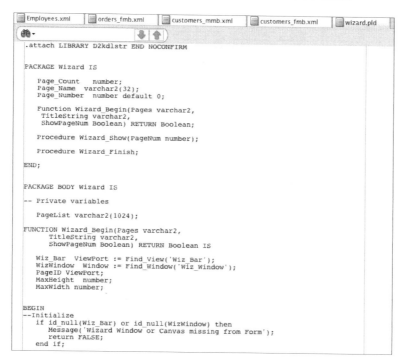

The target database

In order to convert your Forms applications to APEX, we also need the database
model on our target area. Using Oracle's SQL Developer, we will be able to do both
an export and an import on the database of the database objects we need in our
application. In Chapter 1, we talked about the objects we needed in the application
we are converting. The import is also possible in APEX using the SQL Workshop
that is a part of APEX.

First, we will create the `.sql` file, which contains the database objects we need in the application. In SQL Developer we select the objects, in our case the tables, from **S_CUSTOMER** to **S_WAREHOUSE**. When we have selected all the objects, we right-click and select **Export DLL** and then click on **Save to File**, as shown in the following screenshot:

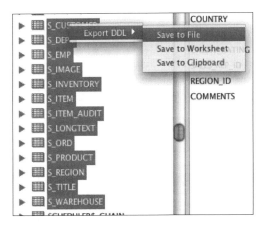

To save the file that contains the code to create the selected database objects, we select the directory where we want to save it, give it an appropriate name, and then click on the **Select** button. After this, the DLL script will be created and saved in the directory we have chosen.

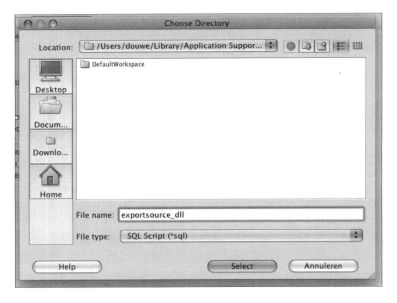

When we get the DLL script of our database objects, we will implement it on our target database. This can be done by using both Oracle SQL Developer and APEX.

First, we will do it in SQL Developer because we will be able to connect this IDE to any database we are connected to, and this works pretty easy with the appropriate user credentials.

We have to open the file we just created. Click on **File** | **Open** (or use the keyboard shortcut *Ctrl+O*). This opens a dialog box in which we can select the file, as shown in the following screenshot:

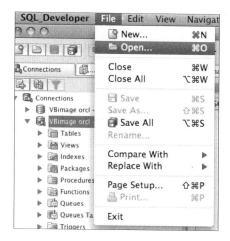

The file will open in a separate worksheet in SQL Developer. Now we can see the statements that create the database objects for which we created the DLL file. At this point, we want to run the script on the target database schema. In the following screenshot, we see the script in SQL Developer.

By pressing *F5* on our keyboard, or by going to **Run** in the menu and clicking on **Run exportsource_dll.sql**, we will run this script:

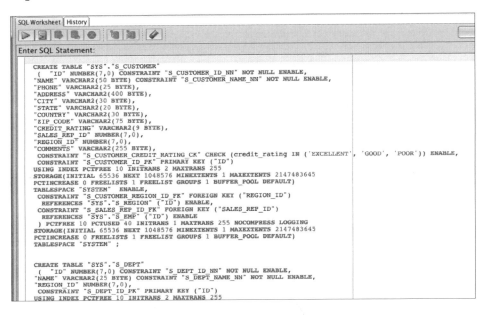

Before the actual run of the script, we need to select a connection on which the script must run. In this example, we will run the script on the OMB database schema that I have saved in my SQL Developer preferences. To learn more about the possibilities SQL Developer offers, it would be smart to read the SQL Developer user guide. After selecting the correct connection, we click on **OK** and the script will run on the selected database schema using the username and password settings we saved. Look at the next screenshot:

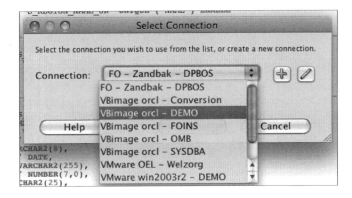

It's also possible to run the script in APEX. This might come in handy if we don't have a connection saved in our SQL Developer settings, or we just don't have the database connection on our computer.

In APEX, we first go to the place where we can control our database objects, which is the SQL Workshop. In the SQL Workshop, we see a section called **SQL Scripts**. In this section of APEX, we can upload, create, save, edit, and run our `.sql` scripts.

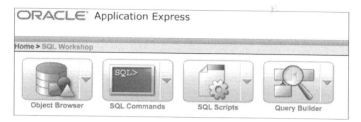

In the **SQL Scripts** section of **SQL Workshop**, we have the possibility to upload our script. Click on the **Upload** button shown at the righthand side in the following screenshot. When we have done this, we browse to the file we created in SQL Developer and give it an appropriate name. In this example, we call it **exportsource**. Now we can upload the file. Click on the **Upload** button to upload the file and we are redirected to the **SQL Scripts** section of APEX.

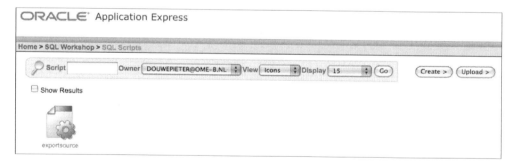

Now, we want to run the script. Click on the script we just created in the **SQL Scripts** section. In this example, we click on the icon that is named **exportsource**. This will take us to the page shown in the following screenshot:

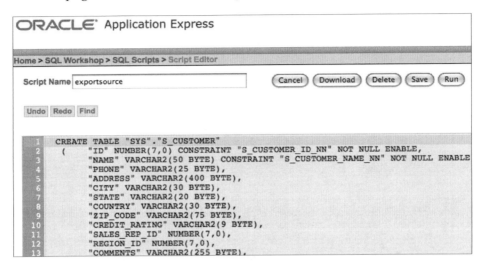

On the righthand side of this screen, there is a button called **Run**. Click on this and the script will run on the same database schema we are connected to as the APEX user.

We can repeat all the steps we took to implement the tables on a target database in order to implement other database objects such as views, procedures, packages, and more.

Summary

In this chapter, we learned everything we need to do to get ready for our Forms to APEX conversion project. Here are the necessary steps we went through before we started:

- We have seen what files we need. These are the .FMB (Forms Modules), .OLB (Object Libraries), .MMB (Menu Modules), .PLL (PL/SQL Libraries), and RDF, REX, or JSP (Reports) files.

- We have used the Forms2XML conversion tool — the rwconverter — and the Reports Builder in Oracle Developer Suite to create the right files that we need for the APEX conversion project. We have used Forms2XML in the command line to convert Forms Modules, Object Libraries, and Menu Modules to XML files. We have seen how to use the Reports Builder to save a Reports File as an XML File. We have also seen how the rwconverter command is used to create a flat file in the PL/SQL Library.

- Using SQL Developer, we have seen what data is contained in the XML files that we created. The XML files contained the same information that we have seen in the Forms and Reports Builder, but is now structured within XML tags.

- We have done an export of our database objects from the SQL Developer, and have implemented these database objects in our target database using the SQL Developer and the Application Express.

In the next chapter, we will use the XML files we created in this chapter to create a Forms Conversion project in APEX. We will upload these files in the APEX conversion tool and get acquainted with the Forms Conversion project in APEX. The project page will be our home page and we will see how we use the information in this project page to edit any project in the future.

3
Create your Forms Conversion project

The XML files we created in the previous chapter will now help us on our way in APEX. During this chapter, we will create our own conversion project in APEX and upload the XML files to the Forms Conversion project. This will also be the first time we see the Forms Conversion project page and will learn a few things such as how to use this to our advantage. Creating the project by uploading the XML files is a hands-on experience because we need to implement the information that is contained in the XML files into the APEX repository.

The following steps will be taken to create our Forms Conversion project:

1. We will create the project in APEX by giving it the appropriate settings.
2. We will upload the XML files we created earlier to the project we just created.
3. We will add additional sources to the project, that is, more XML files such as our menus and libraries.
4. We will see how the project page is used and what information we can find in it.
5. We will learn how to edit the project defaults in the project page and how to set up the project before we start working on it.

Getting started

Before we can upload the XML files and define our application, we will have to navigate to the **Application Migrations** page in APEX. This is a separate section in APEX for all our migrations and because we see Forms Conversion as migration, we need to be here.

In the following screenshot, we see the **Migrations** section which is placed on the righthand side of the APEX home page. To go to this part of our APEX installer, we have to click on the **Application Migrations** link as follows:

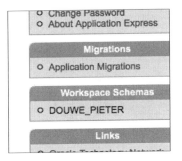

When we get to the **Application Migrations** part of APEX, we see a report of all our migration projects. These can be Access Migrations, Forms Conversions, and so on. But we will go for Forms Conversions as we want to create our very own Forms Conversion project.

To create a new project, click on the **Create Project** button above the report as we see in the following screenshot:

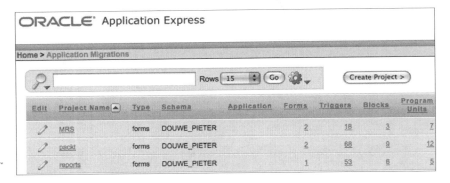

Creating the project

At this point, we are creating our Forms Conversion project in Oracle APEX. First, we need to define a few of the basic parameters such as the name of our project, the type of migration we are doing, and so on.

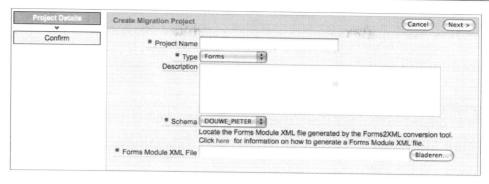

Let's fill in the basics. In this example, we define the following:

- **Project Name**: It is the name of our conversion project. I chose **FormsConversion**, but you can choose a logical name for the project.

- **Type**: In our case, this will be **Forms**.

- **Description**: This describes the project we are doing. We tell in a few words what we are doing in this project and why.

- **Schema**: This defines the database schema that we want our project to be built on. This is the schema that we used to implement the database objects in.

- **Forms Module XML File**: This is the first XML file that we are uploading to the project. This has to be a Forms Module XML file, and is probably saved as a `_fmb.xml` file.

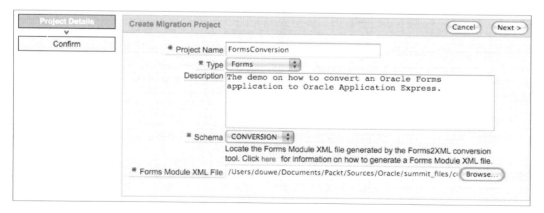

When we have entered the basic information of our Forms Conversion project and selected the first **Forms Module XML File**, we click on the **Next** button to go to the next page. The following screenshot will appear before us:

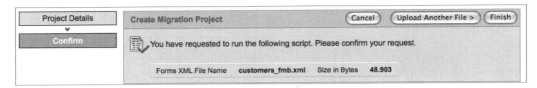

At this point, we can choose to add more XML files to our Forms Conversion project. I decided to do so in our example, but we will be able to add more sources at a later stage. To add more sources at this stage, we click on the **Upload Another File** button. To create the project, we click on the **Finish** button. In the following screenshot, we can see the files we added at this stage:

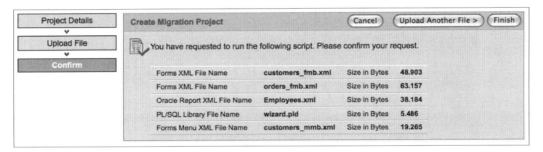

Adding additional sources

When we finish creating our Forms Conversion project in APEX, we get directed to the project page. At this point, we are able to see all the sources that we added so far to our project and we can look into them. But first, we will put more sources in our project. We will add another file to our Conversion project.

To add another source file to our project, let's click on the **Upload File** button above the report as we can see in the following screenshot:

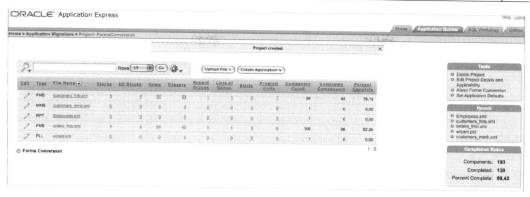

At this point, we just have to define some basics of the file that we are about to
upload to our project. We have to:

- Define the **File Type**: In our example, we will upload another Forms module,
  which is a `_fmb.xml` file. Of course, we can choose the different supported
  types of our Forms Conversion.

- **Browse** for the file: This has to be of the same type as we defined in the field
  above. In our example, we browse for the `C:\summit\customer_fmb.xml` file.

- Click on the **Upload** button to finish uploading the file and add it to our
  conversion project: Instead, we can click on the **Upload and Upload Another**
  button if we want to add more than just one source to the project.

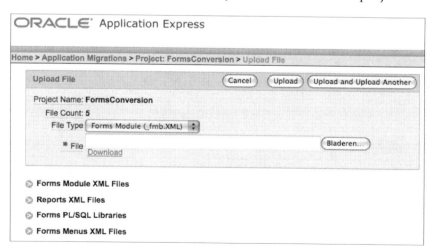

The project page

After we finish adding sources to our project, we can take a further look into the project page. The project page is the home page of our Forms Conversion project and gives us a lot of insight into the elements that we are about to convert to APEX. As the page gives us so much information, we will also use it for managing our project and estimating our progress.

On the project page, we find all the sources with their attributes. The Forms modules that we uploaded as XML files have the most information in them. We get a report with a few necessary information points that can be explained as follows:

- **File Type** means the type of source file we uploaded into our project. The project page uses a three-letter abbreviation of the type of file. For Forms Modules it's FMB, for Reports it's RPT, for Forms Menus it's MMB, and for Libraries it's PLL.
- **File Name** means the name of the file we uploaded into our project. This is the same name we gave it during the conversion to XML.

Forms Modules have a few additional elements in this report that are Forms Module unique. For the other file types, we only see a zero as a value for the quantity of the following elements:

- Blocks
- DB Blocks
- Items
- Triggers
- Record Groups
- Lists of Values
- Alerts
- Program Units

We have a count of the progress of all the files. These fields are useful to help us realize the Conversion project. The following fields are used for the component count:

- The component count: The sum of all the components available in the specific source file.
- The number of completed components: The sum of the components that either have the complete status, or are just not applicable in the project. This has been done during the conversion project and is discussed further in this book.
- The percentage of completion of the file: The completion percentage of a specific file.

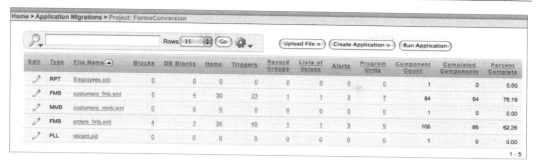

We also have a **Completion Status** of our complete project. This status bar is located on the right of the project page and indicates how much progress we have made. We can see how many components there are in total, how many components have been completed, and what percentage of the project is completed. This is useful information for us to look into once in a while because it will tell us the status of our project. But, beware! There are some components in the Forms Modules we will not be able to complete.

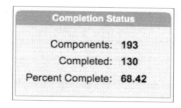

Editing the project

After creating our project, we are able to edit some of its defaults and details. This will come in handy if we want the project page to be the starting point in our project. The things we can edit are the project details, which we entered during the creation of our project—the applicability of the components and the triggers. Besides these details and applicability settings, we are also able to edit the application defaults. These have a lot to do with how we want the application, which will be generated in APEX to react, such as the user interface and the language of the application.

On the right of our project page we see the **Tasks** region. This region contains all the possible settings for editing and setting our Conversion project.

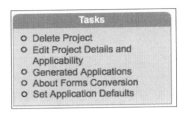

Deleting the project

It's always possible to completely delete a project from the repository. This is done by clicking on the **Delete Project** link in the **Tasks** menu. When we do so, we are directed to the following screenshot:

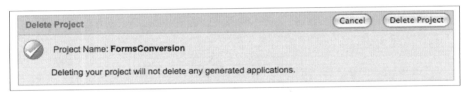

When we click on the **Delete Project** button, the entire project will be deleted from the APEX repository.

Editing project details

To edit the default project details and the applicability of the components and triggers in our conversion project, we have to click on **Edit Project Details and Applicability**. This takes us to the Edit page of our Conversion project. This page is segmented into three main parts—one for editing the project details, one for the applicability of the components found in the Forms Modules, and one for the applicability of the triggers found in the Forms Modules that we uploaded into the Conversion project.

Project details

First, we will see how we can edit the project details. The following screenshot shows us the fields we can edit, and we see that these fields are the same as used in the first page of creating our Conversion project. Here we can edit the **Name** of our conversion project, the **Database Schema** it is set on, and the **Description** of our project.

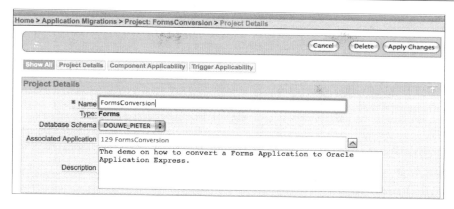

Applicability

Second, we can edit the Applicability of the components and triggers. These applicability settings are the global settings for our project and we see that the values are already set by the development team of Oracle. Applicability means that the applicable components will be a part of the conversion project. If a component is not applicable it will not be part of our project. If it's set to **Yes**, the component or trigger is in the component count and we need to address this particular type in our project. If the value is set to **No**, it is not a part of our project and we don't need to do anything with it. Remember that these are global settings for the complete project, but we can set the Applicability in the component or trigger it as well.

In the following screenshot we see the first components in the list and their Applicability. We can change the Applicability by clicking on the drop-down list and selecting a different value.

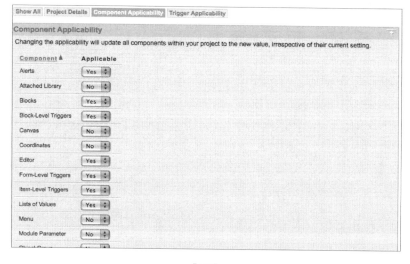

The trigger applicability is a bit tricky because in Forms Modules we have a few different types of triggers such as the Forms-level triggers, block-level triggers, and Item-level triggers. In the following screenshot, we see the different types of triggers and their applicability on Form, Block, and Item level. We can change the values again by clicking on the drop-down lists and selecting a different value.

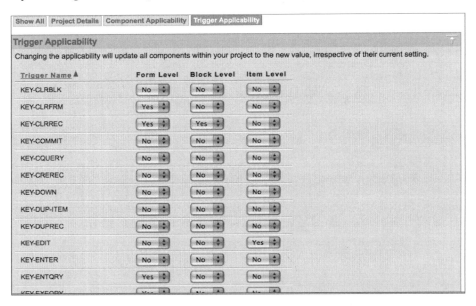

We go back to the project page by clicking on **Cancel** if we made no changes or if we don't want to save the changes we made, or by clicking on **Apply Changes** if we made changes and want to keep them.

Set application defaults

To edit the application defaults, we click on the **Set Application Defaults** link in the **Tasks** region. This takes us to a page in the application builder that lets us set the tabs in the application, the authentication scheme, the application theme, and the language of the application. The application defaults are the settings that are used to know how the application will be generated. It's possible to do this during generation; however, if we think we have to generate the application more often, it's wise to set the defaults here.

Tabs

Navigation through an APEX application is mostly done with the use of tabs. We know two different levels of tabs. In this section of setting the application defaults, we can choose between tabs or no tabs, if that's what we want in our application. **One Level of Tabs** is selected as the default value.

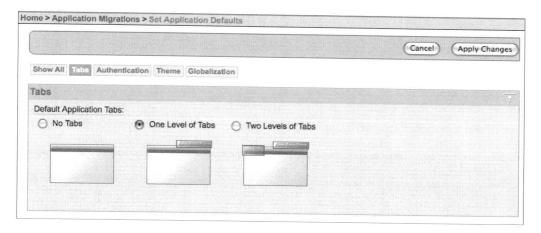

Authentication

We are moving through Forms, so there's a big chance that we have database users and roles in the application that we are converting to APEX. If this is the case, we probably want database authentication. It's also possible to write our own authentication scheme, but I will not go further into this. If we choose the Application Express authentication scheme, there's a big chance that we need to change some settings in our application. But for testing purposes, keeping the settings to default will do.

Theme

In Oracle Application Express, we can choose a theme out of a list of default themes in the APEX repository. These themes can be used for the application that we are generating with our Forms conversion project. Select a theme by clicking on the image, as shown in the following screenshot:

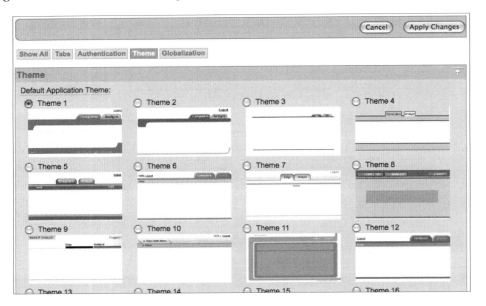

Globalization

The last section in setting the application defaults is used to set the **Globalization** settings. We can select **Default Language** (the way the language is derived) and **Date Format**. It is logical that we can select only those languages that are installed in our APEX instance.

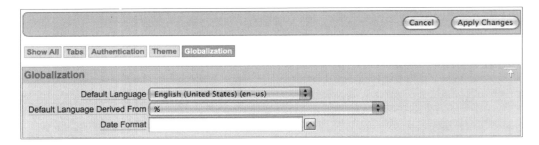

Summary

So, we finally created our own Forms Conversion project in APEX! We saw that it isn't that hard to create it and we got a lot of information from the files we uploaded into the project. The project really comes together now in the project page and we can see how we can do the things that are needed during our conversion project. The following are some important points covered in this chapter:

- We create a Forms Conversion Project by uploading the XML files we build in the Conversion project.

- We always start a Forms Conversion project by uploading a Forms Modules XML file.

- It's possible to make your project larger by adding more sources to the Conversion project. These are also the XML files we created earlier.

- The project page tells us a lot about the components in our Conversion project and the status of our project.

- We saw how we could use the project page to edit the project defaults such as the applicability of components and triggers, and also the user interface and language.

In the next chapter we will learn about the internal aspects of our project. We will see what the possibilities to tie the project together are, how much work we need to do, and what we need to do in order to make this project a success.

4
Planning your Project

One of the largest advantages in using the Forms to APEX conversion in our project is the information it offers us for project management. As a Forms Conversion project is often large and complex, it would be nice if we know what we are talking about and how much work we are looking at.

To determine how much work needs to be done, we will take a further look into the different parts of our Forms Conversion project. In this chapter, we will cover the following:

- In the project page, we will take a look at the count of the different components and the completion of our project
- We will take a further look inside our project and look at the different components inside the XML files that we uploaded
- The most important components in our project will be highlighted and we will see the possibilities to change them
- The component annotations will be used to set the completion status of our project and assign developers
- The annotations are used to give us an insight into the tasks at hand

Overall, we shall see different ways in which we can look into the various components that, combined, is our project. We will also look at how we can edit and estimate the components, and in what way we can have control over our conversion project.

One question that needs to be answered is: Who needs to do what, when, and how much time will it take? In this part of the chapter we will see a few ways to answer this.

The project page

On the project page, we see all the files we uploaded into our project and the components that are in the Forms Modules. This page has a big essence for us, especially when we are planning our project:

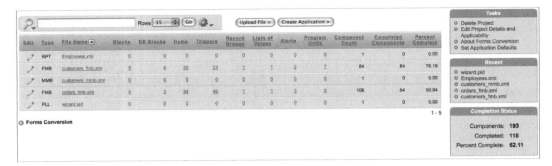

In order to understand what's in our project and how much effort it will take for our team to convert these elements to APEX, we need to take a quick look inside the components.

Inside our project

The number of components that we have in the specific Forms Modules gives us an indication of the amount of effort it will take to successfully convert these modules into APEX. In our example, we have the Forms Module Orders specified in our project as the `orders_fmb.xml` file. In the Orders module, we have 4 blocks, 3 database blocks, 34 items, 45 triggers, 1 record group, 1 list of values, 3 alerts, and 5 program units. This count of components in our Forms Module gives us an indication of the complexity, but it isn't a good perspective.

To know more about the components that our module is built from, we need to take a look inside our project. So let's get more information about these components.

We click on the filename to see a more detailed list of the components the file contains. In our example, we click on the name **orders_fmb.xml**:

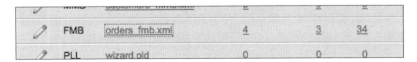

This will take us to the Forms Objects page, as shown in the following screenshot. This page tells us a lot about the components our Forms Modules are built on.

Component	Count	Equivalent Component	Implementation Details	Included	File Name	Applicable
Alerts	3	-	An alert message can be stored as a Text Message in the Shared Components of an Oracle Application Express application. Text Messages can be used to build translatable text strings with substitution variables that can be called from PL/SQL packages, procedures, and functions.	-	orders_fmb.xml	Yes
Attached Libraries	1	-	In Oracle Forms, generic PL/SQL code can be stored in libraries, and incorporated into applications as attached libraries. Such libraries would need to be modified to remove Forms-specific functions and references, in order to integrate them with an Oracle Application Express application either as a PL/SQL page process or package saved to the database.	-	orders_fmb.xml	No
Blocks	4	Regions	A single block can be mapped to a region in Oracle Application Express. Based upon the block type and data source type (table/view) identified in the Forms XML file, some default mappings are defined. For example, a report block which is based upon an Oracle view, will be mapped to an Interactive report in Oracle Application Express. A form block based upon a table, will be mapped to an Interactive report and form in Oracle Application Express.	3	orders_fmb.xml	Yes
Canvas	4	-	In Oracle Forms, the canvas is the object on which the GUI is drawn, the "background" of the form. In Oracle Application Express, the engine constructs the appearance of each page in a application using Templates. Templates define how pages, page controls, and page components display.	-	orders_fmb.xml	No
Coordinates	1	-	Depending on the Coordinate System used in the Oracle Forms application, coordinates can be expressed in real units such as inches, centimeters, and pixels. One unit in an Oracle Application Express item position might not be equal to one physical pixel in an Oracle Forms application. Therefore the coordinate values cannot be automatically applied to the generated application.	-	orders_fmb.xml	No
Lists of Values	1	Lists of Values	A List of Values can be mapped to an equivalent List of Values in Oracle Application Express. When LOVs are selected for inclusion in the migration to Oracle Application Express their associated record group will also be included in the migration.	1	orders_fmb.xml	Yes
Object Groups	2	-	In Oracle Forms, an object group can be defined to package related objects for use in other parts of an application or other projects. Navigation, User Interface, and logic can be easily shared by multiple applications in Oracle Application Express via Shared Components. Also the export/import utility allows for the easy movement of pages between applications.	-	orders_fmb.xml	No
Program Units	5	-	In the post-generation phase of the Forms Conversion process, Program Units can be incorporated into your Oracle Application Express application as a PL/SQL package, page process, computation or validation.	-	orders_fmb.xml	Yes
Property Class	1	-	In Oracle Forms, a Property Class is a named object that contains a list of properties and their settings. An object based on a property class can inherit the settings of any property in that class that make sense for the object. Similarly, in Oracle Application Express, a Theme is a named collection of templates used to define the user interface of an application. Oracle Application Express has a repository of 20 themes, and you can also create your own custom themes.	-	orders_fmb.xml	No
Record Groups	1	-	In Oracle Forms, LOV values are derived from a record group. When an LOV is defined, it is associated with a named record group. When an LOV is included in the migration, its associated Record Group will also be included in the migration to Oracle Application Express.	-	orders_fmb.xml	Yes

The Forms Objects page contains an interactive report with a few elements that we can use in order to plan and understand our conversion project. These elements are discussed next.

Component

A **Component** can be any type of component we know from Oracle Forms. We see **Alerts** and **Blocks**, but also components such as **Windows** and **Canvas**.

Count

Count is the number of component types that are included in this file. In our example, there are three **Alerts** in the Orders Form module. This is the count on the filename level, not the entire project.

Equivalent component

Some of the Forms components we are looking at have an equivalent in APEX. We are converting the pre-existing components to this type of component. For example, blocks in Oracle Forms are considered to be the same as regions in APEX. Not all the components that we get from our Forms Modules are considered to be translatable into APEX elements. This is what makes our job of conversion the challenge it is.

Implementation Details

In **Implementation Details**, we read some text that can help us in making the right choices in the conversion project. This text can be read as a help text that indicates how a certain component is translated to APEX.

Included

In this element, we will see the count of components of the same type that are included in our conversion project. For example, there are four blocks in the `orders_fmb.xml` file, and three of them are included in the conversion project. If we take a further look, we shall see that the one that's not included has its applicability set to **No**. In this way, we see how many of the components will be in our project.

File Name

File Name is the name of the file that the components are in. In our case, this is the Orders Forms Module and so the filename is `orders_fmb.xml`.

Applicable

This element tells us if the components of this type are applicable for our conversion project. In the previous chapter, we saw that we could alter the default project settings per component. These settings are the same as shown here.

For all the types of components we have, some specific settings can be altered and changed. As we will see next, all the components we counted in the project page contain useful information for planning our project.

Now that we know how many components of one type there are, we can make a rough estimate of the complexity of the file we looked at. In this case, it is the `orders_fmb.xml` file. If we look at all the files we have in our project, we can make an estimate of the entire project.

What we need to do

When we make an estimate of the amount of effort it will take us to do our conversion project, we might need more information about the complexity of the components we will be dealing with. We will take a look at the different key components in our project and how the conversion project will treat them.

The Forms Objects list that we discussed earlier tells us a lot about the number of components we are dealing with. This page will be the starting point of the journey towards more information about the complexity of our project.

We will only look further at the components that really count for our conversion project. These are the same components that are stated in our project page, namely, Blocks, Triggers, Lists of Values, Alerts, and Program Units.

Blocks

One of the most important types of components in our Forms Conversion project are Blocks. They can be Database Blocks, but they don't have to be. The blocks we are looking at can contain items and they will be shown here.

In **Implementation Details**, the following is stated about the Blocks components:

A single block can be mapped to a region in Oracle Application Express. Based upon the block type and data source type (table/view) identified in the Forms XML file, some default mappings are defined. For example, a report block which is based upon an Oracle view, will be mapped to an Interactive report in Oracle Application Express. A form block based upon a table, will be mapped to an Interactive report and form in Oracle Application Express.

As we read the **Implementation Details**, we learn that a **Block** is defined as a region in APEX. We also learn that the way a region will be defined in our conversion project has a lot to do with the way the original Block was defined in Oracle Forms. For example, if the Block was defined as a report Block, we will generate an Interactive Reports region in APEX. The query the Block is based on is probably it's most important aspect.

When we click on the **Blocks** link on the Forms Objects page, we will be taken to the page that reports all the Blocks in this file to us, as shown in the following screenshot:

Include	Name	Title	Triggers	Data Source Name	Item Count	Database Block	Update Allowed	Insert Allowed	Records Display Count	Applicable	Complete	File Name
☑	Orders	Orders	22	S_ORD	9	Yes	Yes	Yes	1	Yes	No	orders_fmb.xml
☑	Items	Items	8	S_ITEM	11	Yes	Yes	Yes	4	Yes	No	orders_fmb.xml
☑	Inventories	Inventories	0	S_INVENTORY	6	Yes	Yes	Yes	4	Yes	No	orders_fmb.xml
☐	Controls	Controls	8		8	No	Yes	Yes	1	No	Yes	orders_fmb.xml

1 - 4

At this point, we can edit the defaults of our Blocks and thus learn some more about the way our Blocks are built. Amongst the important information we can see in our example is that our **Orders** block contains **22 Triggers** and that the name of the data source is **S_ORD**, which has **9 Items** and is a **Database Block**.

If we look further in the Block, we can see more details. To see more information about this Block, we need to click on the name of the Block we want to look at. In our example, we take a look at the **Orders** Block. Clicking on this name takes us to the following screenshot:

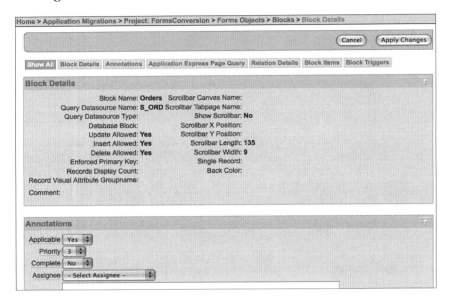

In the previous screenshot, we can change the most important settings and values. In the following screenshot, we can see the query, relation details, items on this block, and the block-level triggers. By looking into the information about the Block, we can estimate more accurately how much time it will take for us to completely convert this element from Forms to APEX.

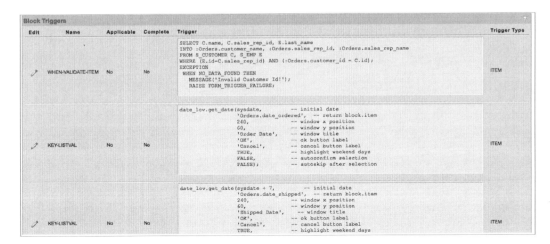

The triggers in this Block can be edited directly by clicking on the pencil icon in front of the **Trigger** name.

Triggers

Triggers are probably the most complex part of our conversion project. As we have to take account of a lot of these triggers with their own logic and importance, we need to spend some time investigating them.

Our application contains a large number of different triggers of all sorts and types. Let's take a look at the triggers in Forms Module Orders that we uploaded into our project as orders_fmb.xml.

In the Forms Objects page we see the triggers listed. As we can see, the Orders Forms Module contains a total of 45 triggers. This is definitely the bulk of all components in our project.

The **Implementation Details** contain some examples of the way triggers need to be embedded in our project. They are as follows:

An Oracle Forms trigger is an event handler written in PL/SQL to augment the default processing behavior. The trigger logic can be incorporated into an Oracle Application Express application as a computation, validation, or PL/SQL process at post-generation phase. Where feasible, POST-QUERY block trigger logic can be automatically incorporated in the generated Oracle Application Express application, as part of the Enhanced Query generation.

As we have all these different levels and types of triggers in our application, it's difficult to state one way to work with a trigger in our project. Now let's take a look at the different triggers. Click on the **Triggers** link on the Forms Objects page and you will see the following:

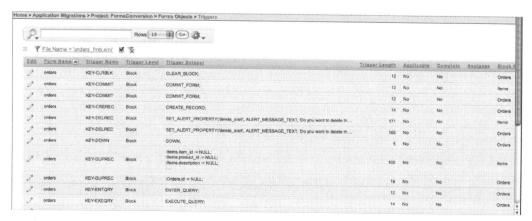

We now see a large list having 45 entries of triggers in this Forms Module. There are other types of triggers and we see the following information on our screen:

- The Form's Name
- The name of the Trigger in question
- The level the Trigger is in
- A snippet of the code inside the Trigger
- The length of the Trigger in characters
- An indication of whether the Trigger is applicable
- An indication of whether conversion of the Trigger is completed
- The name of the developer that got assigned to the Trigger
- The name of the Block the Trigger is on, if it's a Block level trigger
- The name of the Item that the Trigger is associated with, if it's an Item level trigger
- If there are notes combined with this Trigger, a snippet of it is stated
- The name of the file the Trigger comes from

In this case, we work with different levels of triggers. In the interactive report, we can select the different levels and work further from there. As we can see in the following screenshot, we have **Block**, **Form**, and **Item Trigger Level**:

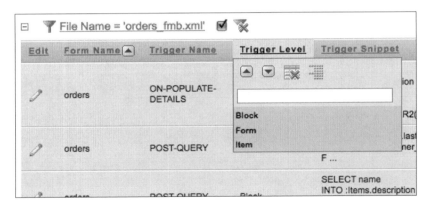

To examine a trigger in more detail, we need to click on the **Edit** link in front of the trigger in the interactive report. To do this, we will click on the pencil icon in front of the trigger that we want to examine. This will take us to the **Block Trigger Details** screen as we see here:

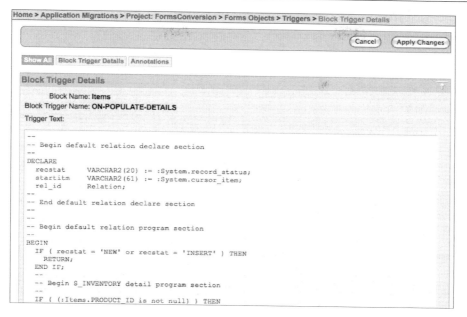

In the above screenshot we can see the details of the **ON-POPULATE-DETAILS** trigger on the **Items** Block. As we can see, this is a Block level trigger. We can look into the text that the trigger contains and we have the possibility to alter the annotations.

Lists of Values

Another type of component that we should take a better look at is the **Lists of Values** (**LOV**s). These LOVs are different in Forms than what they are in APEX. As a lot of applications use LOVs, we will need to know anything more can be done with them than just the automatic conversion.

As we can see in the Forms Objects page, we have one LOV in the Orders Forms Module and there's already one included in our project. As we can read in the Implementation Details, the LOVs and their associated Record Groups will be mapped to APEX LOVs. This means the conversion will be automatic for most parts.

A List of Values (in Apex) can be mapped to an equivalent List of Values in Oracle Application Express. When LOVs are selected for inclusion in the migration to Oracle Application Express their associated record group will also be included in the migration.

Let's take a closer look at the LOV that is in our project. Click on the **Lists of Values** link on the Forms Objects page. This will take us to the following page:

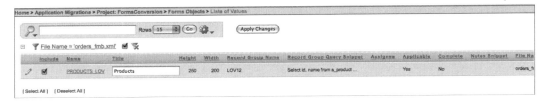

Here we see that the List of Values **PRODUCTS_LOV** is associated with the record group **LOV12**. When we click on the pencil icon in front of **PRODUCTS_LOV**, it takes us to the **Lists of Values Details** page, as shown in the following screenshot:

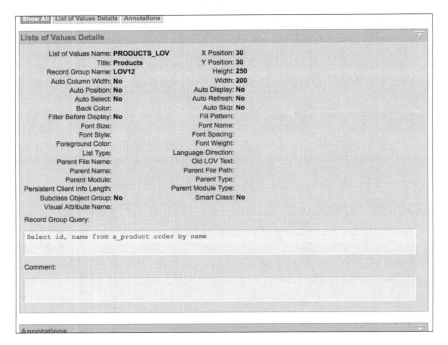

In the above screenshot, we can see the details of **List of Values**. We see that the **Record Group**, which is based on **LOV12**, contains a query. This query will be used as the base for the conversion of this element.

We can also edit the columns that we use in the LOVs. In order to do so, we go back to the overview of the LOVs and click on the name instead of the **edit** link, or the pencil icon. In our example, we click on the **PRODUCTS_LOV** link which takes us to the screen displayed in the following screenshot:

In this page, we can edit the **Column** names and **Titles**. These can be used in order to edit the elements before we convert our application to APEX. In this way we can control our LOVs and the way they are displayed.

Alerts

Alerts in applications give us a special form of functionality. They interact with the user and tell them what went wrong and what went right.

As we can see in the Alerts section of the Forms Objects page of our Orders Forms Module, we have three Alerts in our example. The **Implementation Details** state the following:

An Alert Message can be stored as a Text Message in the Shared Components of an Oracle Application Express application. Text Messages can be used to build translatable text strings with substitution variables that can be called from PL/SQL packages, procedures, and functions.

This means we need to translate the alerts to a text message in APEX. Of course, we need to find out when the alert is given to the user in order to see where we need to implement it in our converted application as a page validation in APEX. On most occasions times, we need to implement the **Alerts** after the conversion.

Click on **Alerts** to see the list of the Alerts in this Forms Module:

In the screenshot above, we see all three of the alerts that are in the Orders' FMB files. We can see the **Name** of the Alert, the **Style** of the Alert (two of them are of the **Caution** style), the labels of the buttons that come with the Alerts, and some additional information.

To edit this information, we have to click on the **Edit** link which is in front of the name. The pencil icon will take us to the **Alert Details** page as shown in the following screenshot. In our example, we click on the **Edit** link in front of the **PAYMENT_TYPE_ALERT** alert.

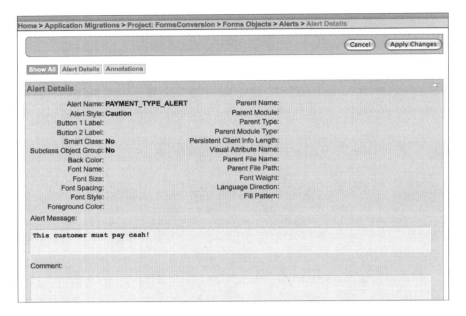

Here we can see **Alert Details** and the **Annotations**. The most important part of information we get from this page is **Alert Message**. In our example, it states: **This customer must pay cash!** So there's probably something wrong with this customer's credit rating.

Program Units

Besides triggers, even Program Units contain code. Mostly, this is the embedded PL/SQL code in the Forms Modules and is used to carry out some functionality.

As we can see in the **Implementation Details, Program Units** have to be implemented after the generation of our converted application. We can see that there are different ways of implementing this kind of logic in our project, so we need to judge every **Program Unit** separately on how we need to implement it later in our conversion project.

In the post-generation phase of a Forms Conversion process, Program Units can be incorporated into your Oracle Application Express application as a PL/SQL package, page process, computation or validation.

Click on the **Program Units** link to take a look at the five program units we have in this Forms Module:

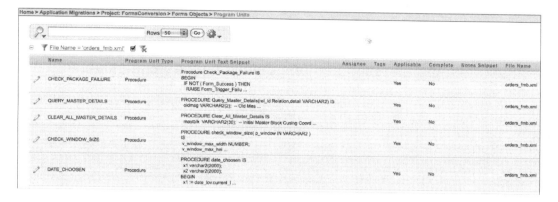

As we see in the previous screenshot, we get some basic information about the **Program Units** in the Orders Forms Module from this page. We see the name of the program unit, the type of Program Unit, a code snippet inside the program unit, and some other basics such as the applicability and the completion of this program unit.

We see that all program units are set to applicable, so we basically need to convert all of them. Let's take a better look at it to be able to judge what we need to do with it. Click on the pencil icon in front of the **CHECK_WINDOW_SIZE** procedure in order to see the **Program Unit Details**. This will take us to the following screenshot:

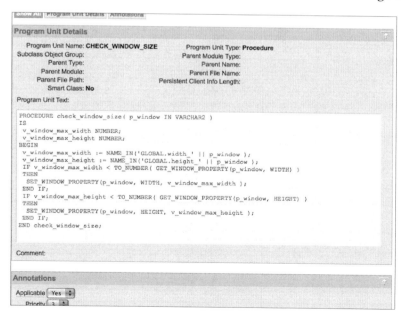

Now we can see the program unit in more detail. The most important part of this screen is the **Program Unit Text**. The example we took in **CHECK_WINDOW_SIZE** is a very Forms-specific procedure and we can safely say that we don't need it in our APEX application after conversion. But we also see that the applicability is set to **Yes**. Can we change this, or do we need to implement the procedure in our project?

Let's talk about the applicability of the components in our project.

Component annotations

In all the **Details** screenshots we have seen earlier in this chapter, we have seen the **Annotations** field. At this point of progress in our project, the **Annotations** field is probably our most important piece of control. We can edit the settings of each component in the **Annotations** field in the details page. As we can see, we can edit a few settings in this part.

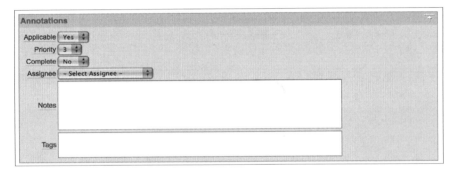

The things we can edit here are:

- The **Applicability** of the component. This is the place were we say if the component needs to be in our conversion project or not.

- The **Priority** of this component. We state how important it is to include this component in our project.

- The **Completion** of the component. After completion, we set this value to **Yes**. This value lets us track the progress of our project.

- The developer that got assigned to and is responsible for this component.

- Some room to make notes about this component.

- What tags there are for the component.

As we can imagine, these fields are very useful to manage our project. Two functions are of essence to us, the status of completion and assigning components. With this information we can control our project and estimate what needs to be done, and how much effort it will take.

Completion status

Besides the applicability on the component level throughout our project, we can set the applicability of each component. As shown above, we can do this in the **Annotations** field in the component-specific sections.

When we take a look at the applicability of some of the components in our project, we can say that we don't need everything in it. In the completion status of our project, we can edit this by providing details of what exactly is in the project.

We saw the completion status in the project page. This is an indication of the status of our project and is built up by dividing the component count through the count of completed components. Because we don't take non-applicable components with the count, we can edit the completion of the project by setting the applicability of the components. In the following screenshot, we see that the completion of our project is now set at **62.11**%. This is not bad for a project that we just started, but let's take a look at the way in which we can edit this using the applicability of components.

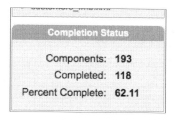

When we change the applicability of one of the components, we change the completion status of our project. Let's change the applicability of the CHECK_WINDOW_SIZE procedure in the Orders Forms Module. We saw earlier that this is a very Forms-specific procedure and we will not need it in our APEX project. In other words, it is not applicable in our Forms to APEX conversion project.

In the **Program Unit Details** page of the CHECK_WINDOW_SIZE procedure, we go to the **Annotations** section. In this section, we find a field called **Applicable** which is set to the default value of **Yes** in our example. We can see this in the following screenshot:

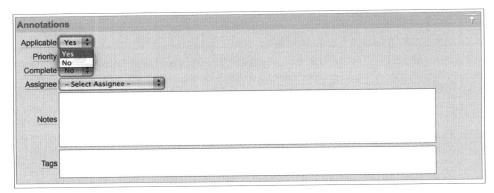

When we want to change the applicability of this procedure, we need to change the **Applicable** field to the **No** value and click on the **Apply Changes** button on the top right of the **Details** page.

When we go back to our project page, we will see that the **Completion Status** section on the right of the project page has been changed. As one more component got the **Completed** status (because we set the applicability to **No**, which the system recognizes as completed), the completion is set to a whopping **62.63**%.

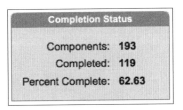

Assign developers

In order to manage our conversion project, we might want to give out work to our team of developers. A really nice feature is that we can assign developers to a certain part or component in our project. In the **Annotations** field in the components or files sections, we not only set the applicability, but we can also assign a developer to a specific part of our conversion project.

If we work with a large team of developers, it will be nice if we could assign different parts and components to our developers. In the **Annotations** field, we can add the developer we want to assign to this part of the project, as seen in the following screenshot. All the developers in the APEX instance that we are working on are shown in the drop-down list. In this way, we can edit our project and assign work to those who might be best for a specific task.

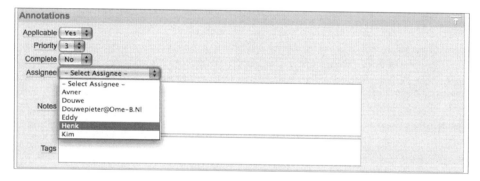

When we have selected the developer who will do this part of our project, we click on **Apply Changes** on the top right of our screen. That's it; we have added the developer.

This feature enables us to manage the workforce in our team. We also get more information on who does what and we might be able to plan the project better.

Project planning

When we do a conversion project, we need to know a few aspects of the project and our team. The most basic question at hand is:

Who needs to do what, when, and how far have we progressed?

 This basic question is probably is one of the hardest parts of our project. So let's look at it in more detail.

Who needs to do what: As we can assign developers to certain tasks in our conversion project, we will be able to answer this question. But we will not be able to fully understand the effort it will take to perform this task. The developer that has the task might be able to tell us, but we don't register this effort in APEX.

When the developer does a certain part of the conversion project, it is another thing we need to record somewhere. But again, it is not possible to do this in the project itself. But because we know what parts are in the project (the parts that are applicable) and who is going to convert them (we assigned a developer), we know the basics to this question.

How far have we progressed is a question that is stated in the **Completion Status** field in the project page. But we will only be able to tell the technical progress that has already been completed. As we all know, 80% of the work is done in roughly 20% of the time. So don't use the completion status as an indication of the work that needs to be done, but use it to measure how much work we already did.

As we are now able to look inside the different components, planning will be easier. The developers who got assigned to a certain component will be able to estimate the amount of effort they need to put in to complete the task and we will be able to plan correctly.

The plus side is that we now know who does what in our conversion project. This means that we have a lot of information that we can use to start the communication lines in the project team. Now that the team knows who has to do what, one of the biggest challenges in the project has been overcome.

Using annotations

The annotations we learned to set earlier can be used towards the project. If we want to know what a developer needs to do, what the progress of a certain developer in our team is, or as a developer what we need to do ourselves, then we can take a look inside the annotations. This can be an extremely helpful part of the project and can be personalized to a great extent.

Here, I will point out a few ways in which we can edit a **Triggers** page in a Forms Conversion project. This can be done with every overview of components and is just an example of the many existing possibilities.

Applicability and completeness

If we take a look inside the **Triggers** page in the Forms Objects, we see that there are a lot of them. In my example, we got a total of 68 triggers. And, of course, this is just an example. In a real live project, this can easily be hundreds.

This means we don't have a good overview of everything, which we ourselves need to have in a large-scale project. So, we need to extend our criteria a bit. For the SQL'ers in our midst, we need to expand our *where* clause. As the **Triggers** page is based on an interactive report in APEX, we can do this ourselves. The possibilities are endless, but let's start by selecting the Triggers that need to be completed.

To select the triggers that need to be completed we need to set filters on two fields in our interactive report. Both the **Applicable** and **Complete** fields are of interest to us in this part of the selection. We used the **Annotations** field earlier to set the applicability of the component. The completeness is also in this field and we can edit it.

To set filters on the **Applicable** and **Complete** fields of the interactive report, we click on the header, in this case on the word **Applicable** on top of the report. This will show the selection we are able to make in this field as shown in the following screenshot:

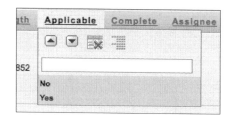

This shows us that we can select between triggers that are applicable and triggers that are not. Because we want the triggers that we still need to complete for our project, we want the triggers that are applicable. In this case, we select the value **Yes**. This is not the only filter we want to set. We only want the triggers that are not already completed.

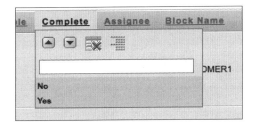

This works in the same way. We click on the **Complete** header in our interactive report and now we select the value **No**. At this point, we have all the triggers in our project that still need to be dealt with. In other words, we got the triggers in our project that are applicable and not yet completed. As shown in the following screenshot, we have set the filters in the interactive report:

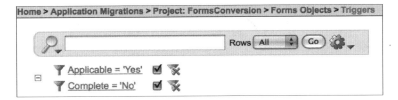

Assignees

So, now we have a selection of triggers in our project that still need some work done on them. If we are in a very large conversion project, this can mean around hundreds of them. In our example, we want the triggers that are assigned to me and the triggers that I need to work on. My team leader has set the assignment of some of the triggers to my name, so I will be able to select them in this interactive report.

I can select the components that are assigned to me by setting another filter on the interactive report. This is done in the same way that we have set the applicability and completeness filters. We will click on the **Assignee** header in our interactive report and see all the developers that have got a trigger assigned to them:

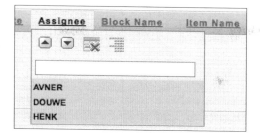

I selected the value **DOUWE** and I will see only the Triggers that got assigned to me and that still need some work done!

Tags

To further limit the selection of triggers in our example, we can use a very helpful element in the **Annotations** field — Tags. **Tags** can be determined as keywords that you, or your team leader, have put in the **Annotations** field and define the component. This can be anything. I choose to use some keywords that are common in the triggers that I saw in the list. There were quite a few that set properties in my Forms application, so I have set a tag called **Properties** earlier.

Tags are not included in the interactive report by default. When we edit the interactive report by clicking on the *radar* image on top of the interactive report, we have an option to select the columns we want in the report. This is shown in the following screenshot:

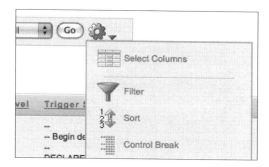

When we click on the **Select Columns** link in the drop-down list, we get a so-called shuttle list where we can select the columns we want in the interactive report. We can select the **Tags** column as shown in the following screenshot:

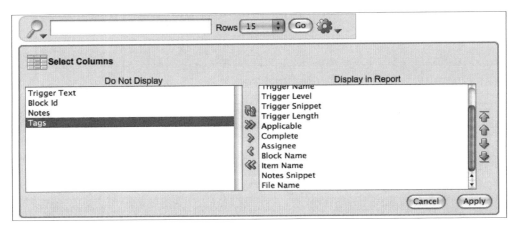

To select the **Tags** column, we click on it and then we click on the single arrow to the right (>). This will put the **Tags** field in our interactive report and we will be able to set a filter on it to make our selection even more accurate. This is done in exactly the same way as is done with the other filters.

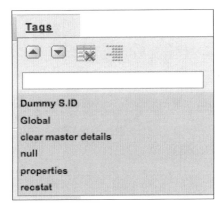

Summary

In this chapter, we saw how we can use the information given to us in the conversion project to our advantage. We have seen how we can look into components that are in the conversion project and what information is given to us.

To entirely plan a Conversion Project, we are handed a few functions that help us understand and control the project. They are given as follows:

- The project page helps us by telling about the amount of components and the completion of the different parts.

- The Forms details screen tells us what to do with certain components by giving us hints in the **Implementation Details**.

- The Forms details screen tells us how many parts of the components there are and what their status is.

- The details of the components and their parameters are given to us in the overviews of every component we have in a Forms Module.

- In the details screen of the specific components, we can take a look at the source and make changes in the annotation of this component.

- The annotations give us some tools to control the page. We can make or unmake the applicability of a component and assign a component to someone in our team.

In the next chapter, we will take a look at some ways to understand and edit the code inside the components in our project page. This means we shall take a step further towards converting our Forms application to Oracle APEX!

5
Getting your Logic Right!

In the previous chapters we have seen various steps needed to create and manage a conversion project. Now let's get ready for conversion and generation itself. This, unfortunately, doesn't mean we're almost there. There's still a lot of work that needs to be done. But don't get disappointed; we are now getting to the part that will earn us money. In this part of our conversion project, we will investigate, analyze, and adjust some of the most important parts of our application. This means that we will set everything up for the generation of the application. We will discuss the following parts of the conversion project in this chapter:

- Investigating the components that will be generated
- Getting to know the database blocks in our Forms files
- Looking deeper into the block items inside our blocks and editing them
- Enhancing the queries on which our blocks are based
- Analyzing the triggers we have in the Forms XML files
- Massively changing the completeness and applicability of triggers or items
- Customizing the query that the blocks are based on in order to complete our generation
- Understanding the way our pages will be generated in APEX
- Editing the titles of our blocks and items
- Analyzing our business logic (probably the most important part)

Pre-generation editing

After reading this chapter, we will understand our project a lot better. Also, to a certain level, we will be able control the way our application will be generated. Generation is often performed more than once as you refine the definitions and settings between iterations.

In this chapter we will learn a lot of ways to edit the project in order to generate optimally. But we must understand that we will not cover all the exceptions in the generation process. If we want to do a real Forms to APEX conversion project, it will be very wise to carefully read the help texts in the *Migration Documentation* provided by Oracle in every APEX instance—especially the appendix called *Oracle Forms Generation Capabilities and Workarounds*, which will help you to understand the choices that can be made in the generation process. The information in these migration help texts tells us how the different components in Oracle Forms will be converted in APEX and how to implement business logic in the APEX application. For example, when we take a look at the **Block to Page Region Mappings**, we learn how APEX converts certain blocks to APEX regions during conversion.

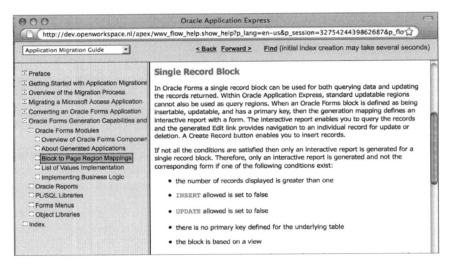

Investigating

When we take a look at our conversion project, we must understand what will be generated. In case of generation, the most important parts are the blocks on our Forms modules. These are, quite literally, the building blocks our pages in APEX will be based upon. Of course, we have our program units, triggers, and much more; but the pages that are defined in the APEX application (which we put in production after the project is finished) will be based on **Blocks**, **Reports**, and **Menus**. This is why we need to adjust them before we generate anything. This might seem like a small part of the project as we look at the count of all the components in our project page, but that doesn't make it less important.

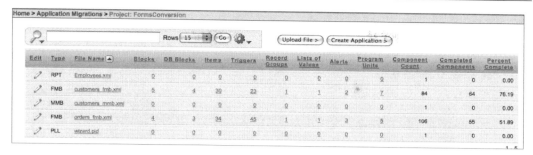

We can't adjust reports as they are defined by the query that they are built upon, but we can alter the blocks. That's why we focus on those components first.

Data blocks

The building blocks of our APEX pages are the blocks and, of course, the reports. The blocks we can generate in our project are the ones that are based on database block. Non-database blocks such as those that hold menus and buttons are not generated by default, as they will be generated as blank pages. In the block overview page, we get the basic information about the blocks in our project. The way the blocks will be generated is determined by APEX based on the contents, the number of items on the block, and, most importantly, the number of records displayed. For further details on the generation rules, refer to the *Migration Guide – Appendix A: Forms Generation Capabilities and Workarounds.*

In the **Blocks** overview page in our conversion project, we notice that not all the blocks are included. In other words, they aren't checked to be included in the project. This is because they are not oriented from a database block. To include or exclude a block during generation, we need to check or uncheck the specific block. Don't confuse this with the applicability of a block.

We also might notice that some of the blocks are already set to complete. In our example we see that the **S_CUSTOMER1** and **S_CUSTOMER** blocks are set to complete. If we take a look inside these components and check the annotations, they are indeed set to complete. There's also a note set for us. As we see in the following screenshot, it states **Incorporating Enhanced Query**:

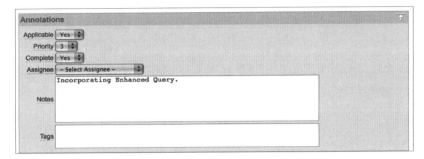

The **Enhanced Query** is something that we will use later in this chapter. But beware of the statement that a component is **Complete** as we will see that we might want to alter the query on which the customer's block is based.

If we look at a block that is not yet set to complete in the overview page (such as the **Orders** block) and we look at the **Application Express Page Query** region in the details screen, we see that only **Original Query** is present. This is the query that is in the original Forms XML file we uploaded earlier.

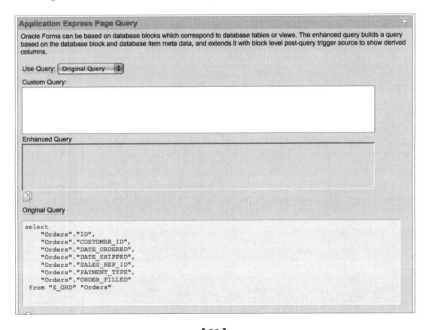

Although we have the **Original Query** present in our page, we can also alter it and customize the query on which this block is based. But this will be done later in the chapter. In this way, we have a better control over the way we will generate our application. We can't alter this query as it is to be implemented as a Master-Detail Form.

Block items

Each block contains a number of items. These items define the fields in our application and are derived from our Forms XML files. In the block details pages, we can find the details of the items on the particular block as well. Here we can see the most basic information about the items, namely their **Type**, **Prompt**, **Column Name**, and the **Triggers** on that particular item. We can also see the **Name** of the item if it is a **Database Item** and if the item is **complete** or not, and whether or not it is **Applicable**. When a block is set to complete, it is assumed that we have all the information required about the items, as we see in the example shown here:

Block Items

Edit	Item Type	Item Prompt	Column Name	Triggers	Database Item	Name	Complete	Applicable
✎	Text Item	Id	ID	0	Yes	ID	Yes	Yes
✎	Text Item	Name	NAME	0	Yes	NAME	Yes	Yes
✎	Text Item	Phone	PHONE	0	Yes	PHONE	Yes	Yes
✎	Text Item	Address	ADDRESS	0	Yes	ADDRESS	Yes	Yes
✎	Text Item	City	CITY	0	Yes	CITY	Yes	Yes
✎	Text Item	State	STATE	0	Yes	STATE	Yes	Yes
✎	Text Item	Country	COUNTRY	0	Yes	COUNTRY	Yes	Yes
✎	Text Item	Zip Code	ZIP_CODE	0	Yes	ZIP_CODE	Yes	Yes
✎	List Item	Credit Rating	CREDIT_RATING	0	Yes	CREDIT_RATING	Yes	Yes
✎	Text Item	Sales Rep Id	SALES_REP_ID	0	Yes	SALES_REP_ID	Yes	Yes
✎	Text Item	Region Id	REGION_ID	0	Yes	REGION_ID	Yes	Yes
✎	Text Item	Comments	COMMENTS	1	Yes	COMMENTS	Yes	Yes
✎	Text Item	Sales Rep Name	-	0	No	SALES_REP_NAME	Yes	Yes

1

1 - 13

But there are also cases where we don't get all the information about the items we want. In our case, we might want to customize the query the block is based on or define the items further. We will cover this later in the chapter.

	Edit	Item Type	Item Prompt	Column Name	Triggers	Database Item	Name	Complete	Applicable
Block Items									
	✎	-	Customer Name	-	0	No	CUSTOMER_NAME	No	Yes
	✎	Text Item	Order Id	-	0	Yes	ID	No	Yes
	✎	Text Item	Customer Id	-	1	Yes	CUSTOMER_ID	No	Yes
	✎	Text Item	Date Ordered	-	1	Yes	DATE_ORDERED	No	Yes
	✎	Text Item	Date Shipped	-	1	Yes	DATE_SHIPPED	No	Yes
	✎	Text Item	Sales Rep Id	-	0	Yes	SALES_REP_ID	No	Yes
	✎	-	Sales Rep Name	-	0	No	SALES_REP_NAME	No	Yes
	✎	Radio Group	Payment Type	-	1	Yes	PAYMENT_TYPE	No	Yes
	✎	Check Box	-	-	0	Yes	ORDER_FILLED	No	Yes
					4				
									1 - 9

In the above screenshot we notice that for all the items the **Column Name** is not known. This is an indication that the items will not be generated properly and we need to take a further look into the query and, maybe, some of the triggers.

When we want to alter the completeness and applicability of the items in our block, there's a great functionality available on the upper-right of the **Blocks Details** page. In the **Block Tasks** section, we find a link that states: **Set All Block Items Completeness and Applicability**. This function is used to make bulk changes in the items in the block we are in. It can be useful to change the completeness of all items when we are not sure what more needs to be done.

To set the completeness or the applicability with a bulk change on all the items, we click on the link in the **Block Tasks** region and this takes us to the following screen:

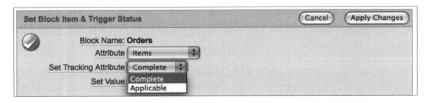

In the **Set Block Item & Trigger Status** page we can select the **Attribute (Items,
Block Triggers,** or **Item Triggers),** the **Set Tracking Attribute (Complete** or
Applicable), and the **Set Value (Yes** or **No).** To make changes, set the correct
attribute, tracking attribute, and value, and then click on **Apply Changes.**

Original versus Enhanced Query

As mentioned earlier, we can encounter both **Original** and **Enhanced Queries** in
the blocks of our Forms. The **Original Query** is taken from the XML file directly as
it is stated in the source of the block we are looking at. So where does the **Enhanced
Query** originate from? This is one of the automatically generated parts of the Forms
Conversion tool in APEX. If a block contains a **POST QUERY** trigger, the Forms
Conversion tool generates an **Enhanced Query** for us.

In the following screenshot, we see both the **Enhanced Query** and the **Original
Query** in the **S_CUSTOMER** block. We can clearly notice the additional lines at
the bottom of the **Enhanced Query.**

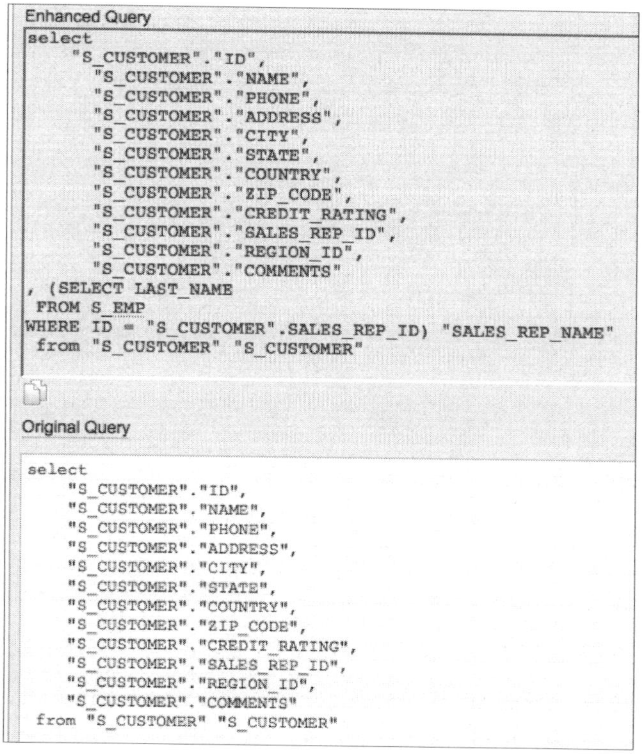

The query in the **Enhanced Query** section still looks a lot like the one in the **Original Query** section, but is slightly altered. The code is generated automatically by taking the code from both the **Original Query** and **POST QUERY** triggers on this block. Please note that the query is automatically generated by APEX by adding a **WHERE** clause to the SQL query. This means that we will still need to check it and, probably, optimize it to work properly.

The following screenshot shows us the **POST QUERY** trigger. Notice that it's set to both applicable and complete. This is because the code is now embedded in the enhanced query and so the trigger is taken care of for our project.

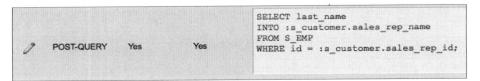

```
SELECT last_name
INTO :s_customer.sales_rep_name
FROM S_EMP
WHERE id = :s_customer.sales_rep_id;
```

Triggers

Besides items, even blocks contain triggers. These define the actions in our blocks and are, therefore, equally important. Most of the triggers are very Forms-specific, but it's nice to be the judge of that ourselves.

In the **Orders Block**, we have the **Block Triggers** region that contains the triggers in our orders block. The region tells us the name, applicability, and completeness. It gives us a snippet of the code inside the trigger and tells us the level it is set to (**ITEM** or **BLOCK**).

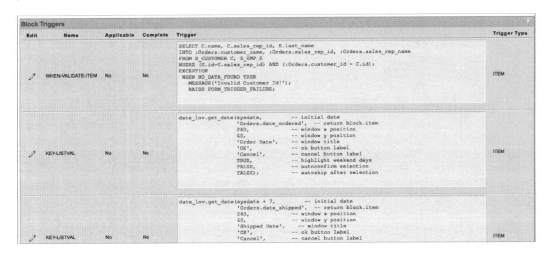

A lot of the triggers in our project need to be implemented post-generation, which will be discussed later in this chapter. But as mentioned above, there is one trigger that we need in the pre-generation stage of our project. This is the **POST-QUERY** trigger.

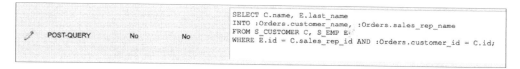

In this example, the applicability in the orders block is set to **No**. This is also the reason why we have no **Enhanced Query** to choose from in this block. The reasons behind setting the trigger to not applicable can be many, and you can learn more about the reasons if you read the migration help texts carefully.

We probably want to change the applicability of the trigger ourselves because the **POST QUERY** trigger contains some necessary information on how we need to define our block. If we click on the edit link (the pencil icon) for the **POST QUERY** trigger, we can alter the applicability.

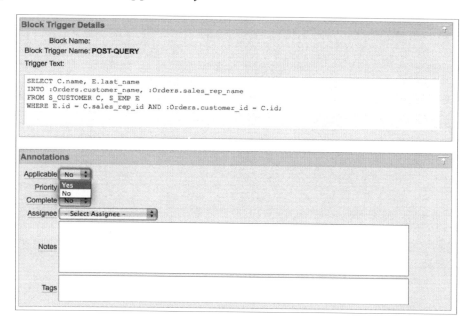

Set the value for **Applicable** to **Yes** and click on **Apply Changes**. This will take us back to the **Block Details** screen. In the **Triggers** region, we can see that the applicability of the **POST QUERY** trigger is now set to **Yes**.

🖉	POST-QUERY	Yes	No	`SELECT C.name, E.last_name`
				`INTO :Orders.customer_name, :Orders.sales_rep_name`
				`FROM S_CUSTOMER C, S_EMP E`
				`WHERE E.id = C.sales_rep_id AND :Orders.customer_id = C.id;`

Now if we scroll up to the **Application Express Page Query** region, we can also see that the **Enhanced Query** is now in place. As shown in the following screenshot, we can see that we automatically generated an extended version of the **Original Query**, embedding the logic in the **Post Query** trigger. For the developers among us, we can see that the query produced by the conversion tool in APEX doesn't make the query very optimal. We can rewrite the query in the **Custom Query** section, which we will describe later in this chapter.

```
Enhanced Query
select
    "Orders"."ID",
    "Orders"."CUSTOMER_ID",
    "Orders"."DATE_ORDERED",
    "Orders"."DATE_SHIPPED",
    "Orders"."SALES_REP_ID",
    "Orders"."PAYMENT_TYPE",
    "Orders"."ORDER_FILLED"
, (SELECT C.NAME FROM S_CUSTOMER C, S_EMP E
WHERE E.ID = C.SALES_REP_ID AND "Orders".CUSTOMER_ID = C.ID) "CUSTOMER_NAME",
(SELECT E.LAST_NAME
 FROM S_CUSTOMER C, S_EMP E
WHERE E.ID = C.SALES_REP_ID AND "Orders".CUSTOMER_ID = C.ID) "SALES_REP_NAME"
 from "S_ORD" "Orders"
```

```
Original Query
select
    "Orders"."ID",
    "Orders"."CUSTOMER_ID",
    "Orders"."DATE_ORDERED",
    "Orders"."DATE_SHIPPED",
    "Orders"."SALES_REP_ID",
    "Orders"."PAYMENT_TYPE",
    "Orders"."ORDER_FILLED"
 from "S_ORD" "Orders"
```

We are able to set the values for our triggers in the same way we used to set the applicability and completeness of the items in our blocks.

In the upper-right corner of our **Block Details** screen, we find the **Block Tasks** region. Here we find the link to the tasks for items as well as triggers.

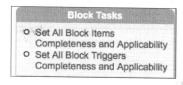

Click on the **Set All Block Triggers Completeness and Applicability** to navigate to the screen where we can set the values. In the **Attribute** section, we can choose from both the block level triggers as well as the item level triggers. We can't adjust them all at once, so we may need to adjust them twice.

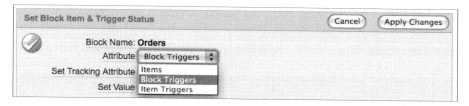

Custom Query

We already learned how we can incorporate an **Enhanced Query** as the base for the blocks in our project, but sometimes we would want to edit or adjust the query ourselves. This is why we have the possibility to create a custom query in our blocks. If the enhanced or original query isn't sufficient, we can enter our own custom query.

It would be strange to build this custom query from scratch, as we can use either the original or, sometimes, the enhanced query as a basis. We are able to copy the code in the **Original** or **Enhanced** query sections to the custom query section. This is done with the copy icon 📄 underneath the **Original** and **Enhanced Query** boxes. In the following screenshot, we see this button in the **S_CUSTOMER** block.

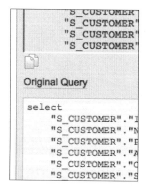

In this example, let's click on the copy icon underneath the **Enhanced Query** to copy this code into the **Custom Query** section. As we can see in the next screenshot, the query is copied into the **Custom Query** field, which we can edit ourselves:

```
Custom Query:
select
    "S_CUSTOMER"."ID",
    "S_CUSTOMER"."NAME",
    "S_CUSTOMER"."PHONE",
    "S_CUSTOMER"."ADDRESS",
    "S_CUSTOMER"."CITY",
    "S_CUSTOMER"."STATE",
    "S_CUSTOMER"."COUNTRY",
    "S_CUSTOMER"."ZIP_CODE",
    "S_CUSTOMER"."CREDIT_RATING",
    "S_CUSTOMER"."SALES_REP_ID",
    "S_CUSTOMER"."REGION_ID",
    "S_CUSTOMER"."COMMENTS"
, (SELECT LAST_NAME
 FROM S_EMP
WHERE ID = "S_CUSTOMER".SALES_REP_ID) "SALES_REP_NAME"
 from "S_CUSTOMER" "S_CUSTOMER"
```

```
Enhanced Query
select
    "S_CUSTOMER"."ID",
    "S_CUSTOMER"."NAME",
    "S_CUSTOMER"."PHONE",
    "S_CUSTOMER"."ADDRESS",
    "S_CUSTOMER"."CITY",
    "S_CUSTOMER"."STATE",
    "S_CUSTOMER"."COUNTRY",
    "S_CUSTOMER"."ZIP_CODE",
    "S_CUSTOMER"."CREDIT_RATING",
    "S_CUSTOMER"."SALES_REP_ID",
    "S_CUSTOMER"."REGION_ID",
    "S_CUSTOMER"."COMMENTS"
, (SELECT LAST_NAME
 FROM S_EMP
WHERE ID = "S_CUSTOMER".SALES_REP_ID) "SALES_REP_NAME"
 from "S_CUSTOMER" "S_CUSTOMER"
```

We are not quite there yet as we have only the enhanced query in our custom query section. We want our own query in the **S_CUSTOMER** block because we don't have all the data selected from the database yet. When we take a look at the block items in **S_CUSTOMER**, we see that the **Sales Rep Name** is in the items, but we don't get it entirely from our query. Both the original and the enhanced query don't select the sales rep's first name from any source in the database.

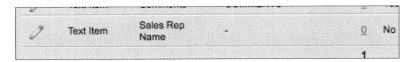

So we need to make some changes to the code we copied to the **Custom Query** section. In this case, the sales rep's first name comes from the **S_EMP** table, which is related to the **S_CUSTOMER** table by the ID of the **Sales Rep.** In this way we can edit the query, so we select the sales rep's first name from the **S_EMP** table and put it together with the Rep's last name in order to get his or her complete name. This query is shown in the following screenshot:

```
Custom Query:
select
        "S_CUSTOMER"."ID",
        "S_CUSTOMER"."NAME",
        "S_CUSTOMER"."PHONE",
        "S_CUSTOMER"."ADDRESS",
        "S_CUSTOMER"."CITY",
        "S_CUSTOMER"."STATE",
        "S_CUSTOMER"."COUNTRY",
        "S_CUSTOMER"."ZIP_CODE",
        "S_CUSTOMER"."CREDIT_RATING",
        "S_CUSTOMER"."SALES_REP_ID",
        "S_CUSTOMER"."REGION_ID",
        "S_CUSTOMER"."COMMENTS",
        "S_EMP"."FIRST_NAME"||' '||"LAST_NAME" "SALES_REP_NAME"
 from "S_CUSTOMER" "S_CUSTOMER",
        "S_EMP" "S_EMP"
where "S_EMP".ID (+) = "S_CUSTOMER".SALES_REP_ID
```

When we're done editing the query the way we want, we need to tell the Forms Conversion tool to use the **Custom Query** when generating the APEX application. This is done in the **Use Query** field. Here we can select the query we want to use during generation. Once you have selected the **Custom Query**, click on **Apply Changes** to save.

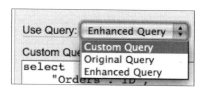

Generation

In the migration help texts, we find a lot of information about how and, specifically, why blocks are generated in APEX. In this part of the chapter we will discuss just a few of them. All blocks that are included in the project will be generated and we will see that it's not always the case that one block is one page in APEX.

For example, let's take a look at the **Orders** block. In the upper-right corner of our details page, we find a field that's called **Block Status**. It gives us information about the block in question and its contents. Here we see that the Orders Block contains **1 Block, 9 Items, 22 Triggers**, that is, a total of **32 Components** of which **21** have been **Completed**. This teaches us that we have a completion of over 65%.

Also very interesting for us at this point is the **Convert As** information in the **Block Status** field. The **Orders** block will be generated in APEX as a **Report and a Form** page. This means that there will be two pages for one block. The main page shall be the report. When we click on the **edit** link in the report, when it's in APEX, we will be taken to the Form to edit the specific row.

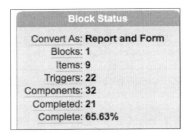

Now let's take a look at a different type of block. This time we are going to investigate the **Inventories** block. When we look at the **Block Status** field, we see that the block has not been completed at all and that it is generated in APEX as a **Tabular Form**:

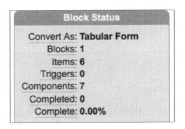

How is this possible and why does the **Convert As** information say it will be generated as a **Tabular Form**?

When we take a look at the **Block Details** section of this block, we see that we are able to update, insert, and delete records using this block. This means that we have a Form on our hands. We also see in the **Records Display Count** that we have **four** records shown in the block. This is the reason why the Forms Converter decides that we need a **Tabular Form**. Makes sense, right?

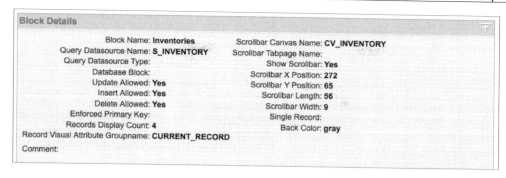

Editing

Before we go and generate our application in APEX, we want to set everything up properly. In our conversion project, we have a lot of nice editing possibilities in place. It's a lot easier to edit the titles and prompts in this phase of our project than doing it afterwards. As we can see in the block overview page in our conversion project, a lot of our blocks have nice, clean titles—but not all of them. The **S_CUSTOMER1** and **S_CUSTOMER** titles from the `customers_fmb.xml` state are not nice titles to have on our page in the APEX application that we are about to generate.

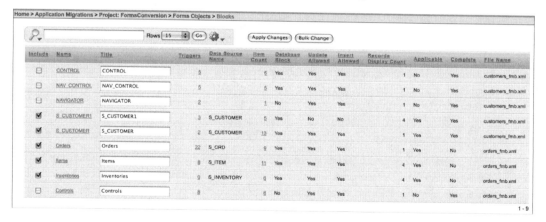

In the blocks overview page, we can immediately edit the **Title** of the blocks. Simply clicking on **Title** for the block in question does this.

In our example, we're going to change the title for the **S_CUSTOMER** block
to **Customers**:

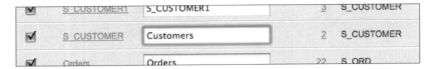

Click on **Apply Changes** to confirm the changes we made in the **Title**. In this
way, you can alter the titles of all the blocks according to your application.

We can also change the titles of all the items on our blocks. In the **Blocks Overview**
page, click on the **Item Count** link. This takes us to the items in this block. In our
example, we take a further look at the items in the **S_CUSTOMER1** block:

This shows us that the titles of a lot of items are not filled in correctly or are not
present at all. You can change them all here by clicking on **Apply Changes** to
confirm the changes we have made.

Analyzing business logic

The most important task we need to do at this stage (pre-generation) of our
conversion project is analyzing what we want to do with all the business logic that's
in our application. We already discussed this in the previous chapter where we
found the logic and looked into the quantity of triggers, alerts, program units, and
more. Now it's time to go into the quality of the business logic in our application.

Implementing the business logic is done post-generation, except for some
Post-Query triggers. At this stage, it's very important to know in what way
we need to implement it before we start generating.

Alerts

One of the features of Oracle Forms is that we have clean alerts that we can set to an action. In this way, the users are given information about the actions they are about to do. It would be nice for the users to know the functionality before they start generating. For example, click on the number of alerts link for the **customers_fmb.xml** file. This takes us to the overview page of all the alerts in the Customers Forms application.

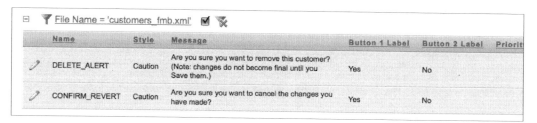

We can implement these alerts in APEX by using some simple JavaScript that creates a pop-up screen in the APEX application containing this alert when a button in APEX is pressed. There is another simple, APEX way to show a red cross with the alert next to an item. In the *Oracle Application Express Users Guide*, there's a section called *Incorporation JavaScript into an Application* that tells us how we need to do this. This is a post-generation step, so for now we're OK. We should update the annotations for each of these alerts with notes, tags, and possibly even assignee.

Program units

Program units can be very Forms-specific. This is certainly the case in our example. One of the most common ways is to implement the program units as application or page processes, but, by and large, this is not the best place to do this. It's commonly preferred to implement program units as a PL/SQL package in the database instead of an APEX application or page process. There's information in the *Migration Help* texts on how we can implement the program units in our application after generation.

It's certainly not always the case that we want to implement program units as a page or application process. Let's take a further look in one example. The **REFRESH_TREE_ SALESREP** program unit in the `customers_fmb.xml` file is quite interesting. If we take a look at the code that's in the **Program Unit Details** page, we can understand why this one might be different.

Program Unit Details

Program Unit Name: **REFRESH_TREE_SALESREP**   Program Unit Type: **Procedure**
Subclass Object Group: Parent Module Type:
Parent Type: Parent Name:
Parent Module: Parent File Name:
Parent File Path: Persistent Client Info Length:
Smart Class: **No**

Program Unit Text:

```
PROCEDURE refresh_tree_salesrep IS
   cursor cursor_sales is
      select   last_name || ' ' || first_name Name, id
      from     s_emp
      where    title like 'Sales%'
      order by title;
   cursor cursor_cust(p_id number) is
      select   name, id
      from     s_customer
      where    sales_rep_id = p_id
      order by name;

   v_i            number := 1;

   rg_custs       recordgroup;

   v_init_state   groupcolumn;
   v_level        groupcolumn;
   v_label        groupcolumn;
   v_icon         groupcolumn;
   v_value        groupcolumn;
begin
   rg_custs := find_group('CUSTS');
   if not id_null(rg_custs) then
      delete_group(rg_custs);
   end if;
```

This procedure creates a tree on the customer's screen based on a few conditions. In APEX, the most logical thing to do is solve this with a database-stored procedure, an application or page process, and some AJAX (Asynchronous JavaScript and XML) components. This, of course, is a real advanced technique and has nothing to do with the Forms Converter. In this way, we can replicate the same functionality in our APEX application. Of course, this is done post generation. You can learn how this is done in the APEX user and developer guides.

Libraries

PL/SQL libraries are basically stored procedures implemented in an Oracle Forms Application. To implement this functionality in the APEX application, we are about to generate a few options. Based on the functionality that's in the PL/SQL Library, we need to analyze what we need to do post generation. Roughly, the possibilities are to create a stored procedure or function in the database and maybe some page or application processes to call them. But certainly, there are more ways to implement this.

For example, let's take a look at the example in our Forms Conversion project. We have already uploaded the **wizard.pld** file to the project. Click on the **PL/SQL Library** link in the project page to go to the **PL/SQL Library Details** page.

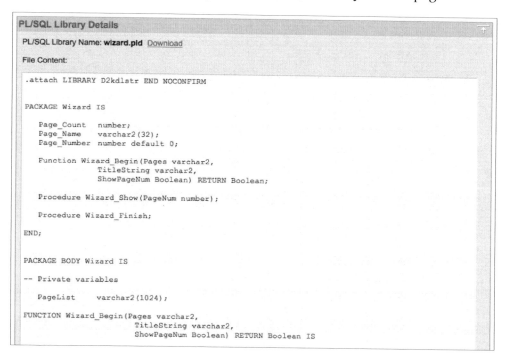

This package has some components that are very Forms-specific. But if we take a further look at the actual code in the package, specifically the **Wizard_Show** procedure, we will notice that there's some functionality in it that we want in our APEX application.

```
-- Enable/Disable Buttons as appropriate
   if Page_Number = 1 then                --first page
      if cursor_loc <> 'WIZ_BAR.NEXT' then
         set_item_property('Wiz_Bar.Next', DISPLAYED, PROPERTY_TRUE);
         set_item_property('Wiz_Bar.Next', ENABLED, PROPERTY_TRUE);
      end if;

      if cursor_loc = 'WIZ_BAR.BACK' or
         cursor_loc = 'WIZ_BAR.FINISH' then
         go_item('Wiz_Bar.Next');
      end if;

      set_item_property('Wiz_Bar.Back', ENABLED, PROPERTY_FALSE);
      set_item_property('Wiz_Bar.Finish', ENABLED, PROPERTY_FALSE);
      set_item_property('Wiz_Bar.Finish', DISPLAYED, PROPERTY_FALSE);

   elsif Page_Number = Page_Count then  --last page
      if cursor_loc <> 'WIZ_BAR.BACK' then
         set_item_property('Wiz_Bar.Back', ENABLED, PROPERTY_TRUE);
      end if;

      if cursor_loc <> 'WIZ_BAR.FINISH' then
         set_item_property('Wiz_Bar.Finish', DISPLAYED, PROPERTY_TRUE);
         set_item_property('Wiz_Bar.Finish', ENABLED, PROPERTY_TRUE);
      end if;

      if cursor_loc = 'WIZ_BAR.NEXT' then
         go_item('Wiz_Bar.Finish');
      end if;

      set_item_property('Wiz_Bar.Next', ENABLED, PROPERTY_FALSE);
      set_item_property('Wiz_Bar.Next', DISPLAYED, PROPERTY_FALSE);
   else                                  --an intermediate page
      if cursor_loc <> 'WIZ_BAR.NEXT' then
         set_item_property('Wiz_Bar.Next', DISPLAYED, PROPERTY_TRUE);
         set_item_property('Wiz_Bar.Next', ENABLED, PROPERTY_TRUE);
```

The code for the **Wizard Show** procedure looks a lot like the "conditional" settings we have on the buttons in APEX. We might want to implement this as conditional buttons in APEX post generation. To be even more specific, we might want to consider doing this on page zero in our application, or the template the application is built on, because this functionality can be used on more than one page. Therefore, it is a general function.

Triggers

The bulk of the business logic in any Forms application comes from triggers. Most of them are Forms-specific and we might not use them in any APEX application because of the basic differences in the way the application is used. Our example isn't any different from this. When we take a look into the **Triggers** section of our conversion project, we see that we have a total number of 68 triggers. This means that we have a lot of functionality that we need to look over to be sure we embed the necessary functionality in our APEX application. If we look at the names of the triggers, we learn that they are very self-explanatory.

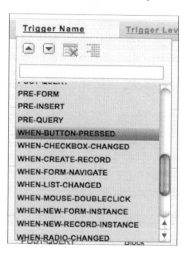

In this example we take a further look at a **WHEN_BUTTON_PRESSED** trigger on the Orders Forms application. Select the appropriate **Trigger Name** in the **Triggers overview** page and take a look at the item-level **WHEN-BUTTON-PRESSED** trigger on the Orders Forms application.

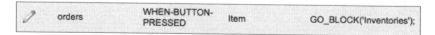

Here we see that the trigger points to another block, the **Inventories** block, on the Orders Forms application. Do we need to implement a page branch after generation? We would probably define a button on the Orders page called **Stock Button**, which branches to the **Inventories** page. Therefore, we should update the annotations accordingly.

These are just examples. Every trigger needs to be evaluated unless the **applicable** is set to **No**. Look into the help texts about Forms conversion in APEX for more information. The appendix of the *Oracle Forms Generation Capabilities and Workarounds* can especially be extremely helpful in order to understand what we need to do with triggers and other business logic in the application we are going to generate that we will discuss post generation.

Summary

In this chapter we learned quite a lot about the steps we need to take before we start the generation of our APEX application. The steps described in this chapter may look quite basic, and in a way they are, but they are very important in order to create a working and functional application after generation.

This doesn't mean we can relax because we saw that most steps have to be done post generation. The business logic has to be implemented in the APEX application to replicate the necessary functionality in the new APEX application.

We did the following steps to prepare ourselves for generation:

- We created the correct query a Block is based on by using the information in the original or enhanced query. With this we created a custom query that collects the necessary data from the database and fills all the items in our block with the correct information.

- We learned how to use bulk changes in the triggers and items to track the progress after generation.

- Editing the blocks and items, especially the titles they work with, was another step we took to make sure the generation will be a success.

- We've taken a look into the business logic in our Forms application and saw some examples on how to implement them after the generation.

- We have learned that a lot of information is in the *Application Migration* help texts in APEX that we can use to determine why and how some elements will be generated.

In the next chapter we will do the actual generation and will finally see some results of the hard work we have done. Are you ready for it?

6
Generating your Application

In the previous chapters, we worked towards this moment. Finally, we are generating our own application from the Forms definitions we uploaded, altered, and looked quite extensively into. We have seen the **Create Application** on the top right of our project page, and at this stage we can click on it. Our patience will be rewarded with a working application at the end of this chapter.

Unfortunately, this doesn't mean that we are there yet; we need to do many more things after generation. It's quite possible that we need to go through the generation process described in this chapter a few more times to get it right. In this chapter, we will learn how we use the settings in our project to create a working application and how we need to change the settings in order to create a working application.

Setting the project

In Chapter 3, we saw different ways to edit the settings in the project. The settings in the **Set Application Defaults** section of our Project are very practical to set pre-generation.

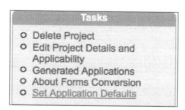

When we take a look at the **Application Defaults** we see that we can change the **Tabs**, the **Authentication** scheme, the **Theme,** and the **Globalization** of the application we will be generating:

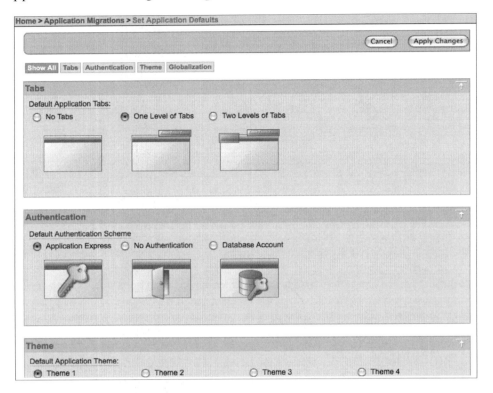

As we can alter these settings in layout and authentication of the application that we are about to generate, we will have better control over the generation process. During the generation steps we need more than just this information, but it will help generate a consistent application.

In this chapter, we will not use the default settings because these can also be determined and set during generation. Besides, we can keep the settings of a generated application once we have done one generation of an application. In this way, we can have our own application design model. We will discuss this in detail later in this chapter.

Start the generation

To start the generation of an application that is based on our Conversion project, we need to click on the **Create Application** button on the top right of our project page. This button takes us to the generation wizard. In this wizard, we tell APEX how we want the application to be generated.

In the following screenshot, we see the first screen of the generation wizard. In this screenshot we can set the basics before we start generating. We can set the name of the application that we want to generate. By default, the application has the same name as the Conversion project however, we can edit the name if needed. This is because we are able to generate more than one application using the conversion project. For this name, it is best to get a name that's logical for the stage we're in. Number the name as you please. As we can see, the **Application** ID is not settable. This ID is assigned to us by the generation process.

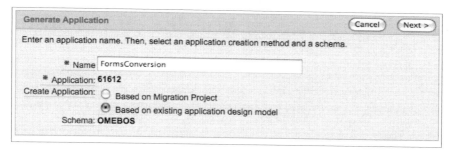

In the **Create Application** section, we have two ways to create the application. We have the option to set it **Based on Migration Project** or **Based on existing application design model**. When we base the creation on the migration project, we use the application defaults we have set in the project ourselves. The existing application design model can be used if we have already created an application in this conversion project and want to refine the output by performing another generation. For our first generation, we need to select **Based on Migration Project**.

Application design models

If we have created an application earlier for our Conversion project, we can use the settings in that application as a design model for applications that we will generate in the future. This means that the layout and authorization is kept for us to use. It's plausible that we need to generate more than once. If we use the application design model from a previously generated application, it means the model will allow us to keep all the formatting and settings we previously set while generating the APEX application.

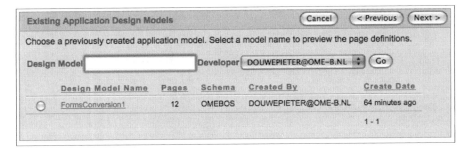

When we have selected the **Based on existing application design model** option in the first screen of the generation wizard, we will get a screen as shown in the above screenshot. This gives us a list of design models from previously generated applications. In this list, we can select a **Design Model** by clicking on the radio button in front of the name. We need to give the design model a name and that's it. We can also select a **Developer** that has developed this design model.

Check the pages

In the following screenshot of the generation wizard, we get an overview of all the pages in our application. Here we can check the settings of these pages and edit them wherever we want. We also have the ability to add additional pages to the project. In this way, we can add pages that we need in the project, but they will not be generated from the loaded source file definitions.

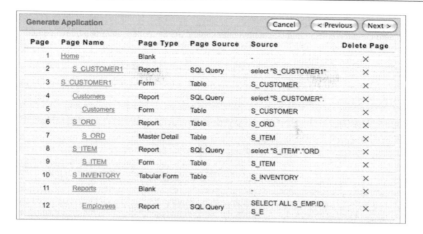

In the overview of pages, we see the page number, name, type of page that will be generated, source type, and source. Only blocks and reports that are included will be listed. Here we are also able to exclude pages from being generated with this application by clicking on the **X** underneath the **Delete Page** heading. When we click on the name of the page, the wizard will take us to a screen where we can edit the details of the page in question.

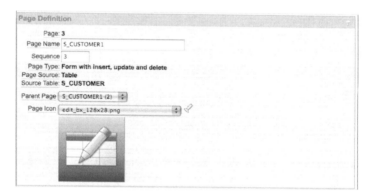

Here we can edit some of the most important parts of the application. We can edit the name of the page, which is generated by getting the title of the Block that it's based on. We can alter the order of the pages here. We can also select a different parent page at this point.

The order of the pages is taken from the Menu file that we uploaded in the Conversion project. The menu is used for the order of pages and the home page in the application are about to generate. In this page, there will be a horizontal list of icons with the name of the corresponding page underneath it. The icon that reveres to the page can be selected in the **Page Icon** section of the page definition. You can change this icon by selecting a different one from the drop-down list, or by clicking on the flashlight icon just on the righthand side of the drop-down list. This takes us to a pop-up screen where we can select a different icon.

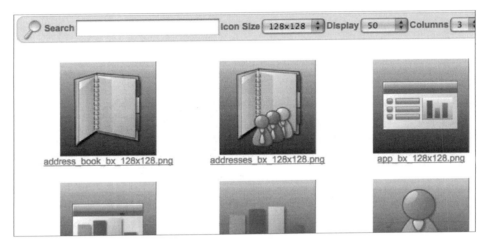

In this pop-up screen, we can select the icon that best matches the page we are going to generate. In this example, we have the Customers page and so it will be nice if we have an icon that matches the functionality of the page. In the pop-up screen, we get a selection of the icons in the images directory of APEX. By default, the images have a **128 x 128** pixels size.

These images will be used to create a home page in the generated application. The images and the title of the page are shown on this home page as a menu to navigate through the application. In Chapter 8, we will talk some more on editing the home page of our generated application.

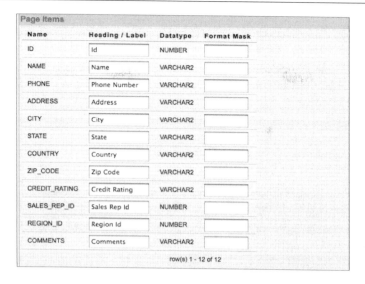

When we get back to the **Page Definition** page, we can also edit the **Headings/Label** and **Format Mask** of the items in the page that will be generated. These are the titles of the Block Items that we have in the Block that this page is based on. During generation, the heading we edit here will be taken instead of the title of the Block Item.

Adding pages

All of the pages in our Conversion project, except for the home page, will be based on the Blocks within the Forms modules or Reports modules. But sometimes, we need to create a new page in the project to add more functionality. Of course, it's possible to add functionality and even pages after the generation of our application; however, to define a good design model for later generation, it might be useful to add the necessary pages to our project at this stage.

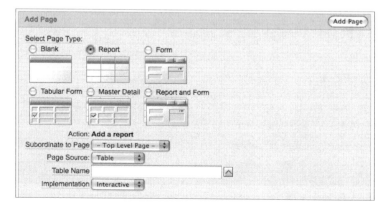

In the **Add Page** section of the **Page Overview** screen, we have the ability to add different types of pages, hierarchy, and page source information.

We can add as many pages as we want to the project at this point. Just select the type, branch it, select the appropriate source, and click on **Add Page**. The page will be added to the list of pages to be generated at the top of this page and can be edited the same as any other pages specified.

Selecting a theme

The next step in the generation wizard is the selection of the theme we want the application to be based on. We get the same choices that we have during creation of a normal APEX application, and by default the theme that we have selected in the Application Defaults settings is selected in the list.

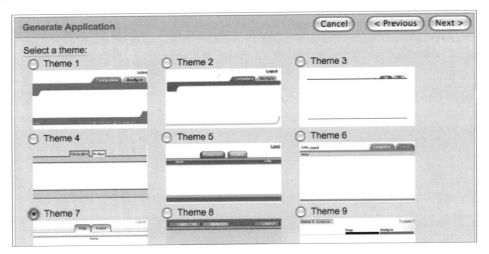

Create the application

The last step in the generation wizard is to actually create ourselves an application. As shown in the following screenshot, here we have an overview of the choices and settings we made in the previous pages in the wizard. If we want to make changes, this is the last stop. Just click on the **Previous** button to let the wizard take you back into the earlier application designing options.

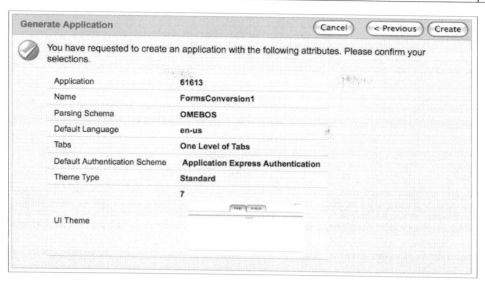

When we click on the **Create** button in this page, APEX will generate an application with the settings we set in this wizard. Nothing is saved before we click on the button, so beware of premature cancelling.

Run the application

To determine if the application is generated as desired, we should now run the application from the confirmation page of the generation wizard. The application will run when we click on the traffic light icon on the confirmation page, as shown here:

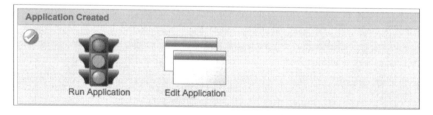

Now, we are taken to the application that we just created. In the following **Home** screen, we immediately see the interpretation of the APEX Forms Converter of a Oracle Forms Menu. The icons are clickable and take us to the corresponding pages in the application.

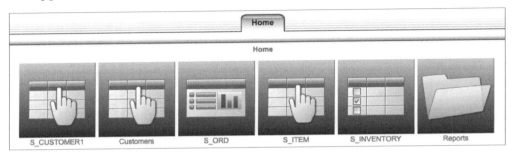

As we can see by the names of the pages, there's still some work to be done. We probably don't want the pages in the application that have names such as **S_ORD**, do we? But this is a different topic.

Summary

In this chapter, we learned how to use the wizard in APEX to create a working APEX application from the files that we uploaded and edited in the Forms Conversion project. The application generation wizard takes us through a few necessary steps in application generation, and we learned how to use these steps:

- We saw how we can use the Application Default settings to our benefit pre-generation
- We learned how to start the generation of an application based on our conversion project and how the settings worked
- We examined the basics of the application design model we can use if we generate an application from this Conversion project for a second time
- We checked the pages in our project and this taught us that we can also make some changes to the order, titles, and headings in the pages we are going to generate
- We saw how we can edit an icon in the home page that functions as a menu in our new application
- We saw that adding pages during generation was one of the possibilities during checking the pages
- We saw how we could define the theme the application was built on
- We generated a first-cut design of providing our first view of the application running in APEX

7
Reviewing and Customizing your Application

Now that we have generated our application, we come to the most important part of our Conversion project—reviewing and, eventually, customizing it in the way we want. As a lot of functionality in the Forms application that we just generated will not be in the new APEX application, we can see that there's still some handiwork to be done.

When we run an APEX application that's generated using the conversion tool, we will encounter a few things that are easily adjusted as well as some parts of the application that need a bit more work. In this chapter, we will learn some ways to adjust and customize the defaults in a generated application.

The home page

The home page in our newly-generated APEX application is based on the blocks which were generated into pages, and not the original menu file (_mmb.xml). When we take a look at the screen, we see a lot of things we need to change. This is done in the page properties within the Application Builder in APEX. In the following screenshot, we see what the home page looks like just after generation:

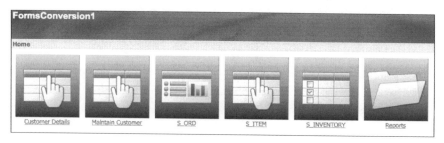

As we see in the home page, we have some names that just aren't that pretty, except for the Block titles that we updated in the project. We need to change some of these names in the **Application Builder**. To do so, we go to the region definition of the **Navigation** region on the first page of our application. Here we see a list with the names and links in the **Source** region, as shown in the following screenshot:

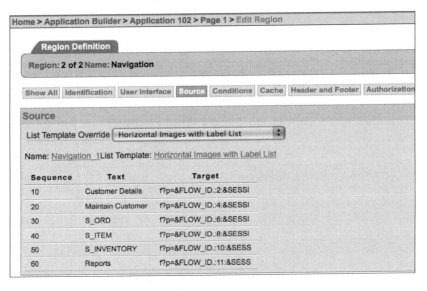

In this **Source** region in the region definition, there is a link to the list that's used to create this menu on our home page. When we click on the list name **Navigation_1** in our example, we go to the following screen where we can edit the names and images used in the home page:

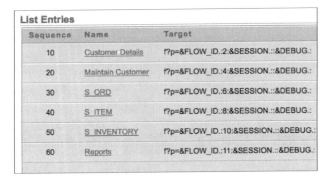

Here, we see the **Sequence**, **Name**, and **Target** page in the application for all the elements on the home page. In our example, we will need to change the names of **S_ORD, S_ITEM,** and **S_INVENTORY** in order to create a good-looking and functional menu on the home page. First, let's change the name of the **S_ORD** menu item. Click on the name and it will take us to the **Entry** field where we can change the name, which is shown here:

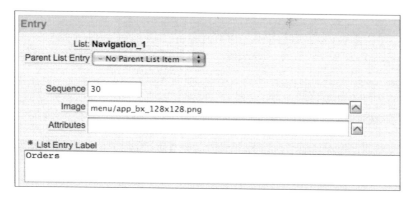

Here we can alter the name of the **S_ORD** menu item to a name we like and which makes more sense to the users. In my case, I changed it to **Orders**. We can also change the **Image** that will be used in the menu, but let's just stick to the name right now. We can also change the names for **S_ITEM** and **S_INVENTORY** in the same way.

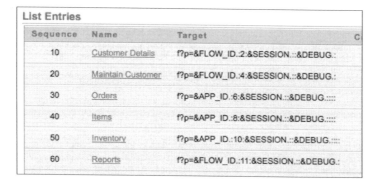

Now when we take a look at the home page, we see that it already looks a lot better than it did before:

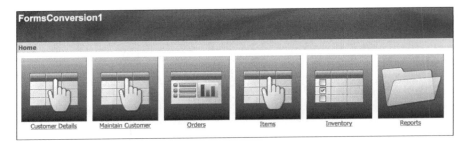

Lists of Values

Now that we have changed the home page and it all looks a bit better for our users, we would like to take another look inside the application to edit the application and make it more functional and useful for the users. First, we will take a look at the functionality in our new APEX application.

In the home page, we click on the link to **Maintain Customer**, which will take us to a report page in which the customers are listed.

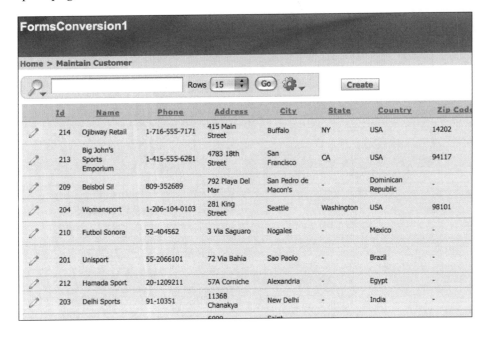

When we click on an **Edit** link in front of one customer, or on the **Create** button, the application takes us to the **Maintain Customer** form as shown in the following screenshot:

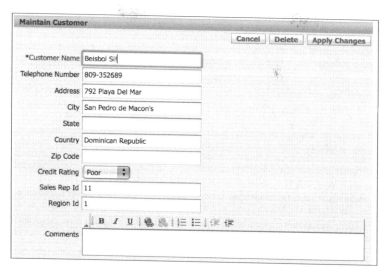

In this form, we need to enter a **Sales Rep Id** to assign a customer to a sales representative. This is, as we can imagine, not entirely functional for users who don't know all the IDs in the system by heart. So let's change this for them.

In the shared components of our application, we go to the **Lists of Values** section. This is shown in the following screenshot:

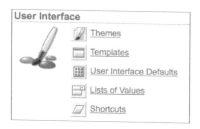

As we already saw in the **Maintain Customer** form inside the application, a **List of Values** exists for the credit rating. Now we are going to create a new LOV for the sales representative. To do this, we click on the **Create** button on the top right of the page.

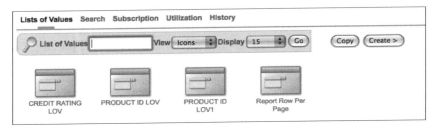

In the create LOV wizard, we will choose to create a dynamic list of values and give it a functional name. In this example, we named the LOV **SALES_ REPRESENTATIVES**. When we get to the page where we can edit a SQL query, we can insert one to obtain the data we need. As we see in the following screenshot, we insert the query to only return these employees in the **Sales** department:

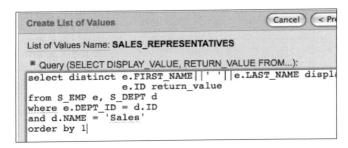

Let's now edit the page containing the **Maintain Customer** form, in our example **Page: 5**, to use a LOV instead of the numeric ID in the form. To edit this functionality, we need to click on the name of the item we want to change in the form. In this case, it is item **P5_SALES_REP_ID**.

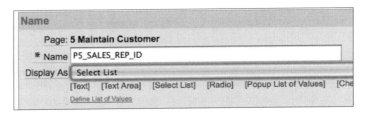

In the **Name** section, we change the **Display As** value from the **Text** field to the **Select List** field. Now we scroll down to the **Lists of Values** section and select **Named LOV SALES_REPRESETATIVES** as the value.

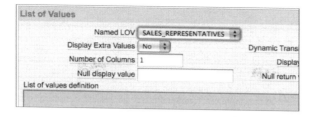

When we run the page, it will look like the page shown in the next screenshot. We see that we created a drop-down list where the user can select the sales representative who's responsible for the customer in question.

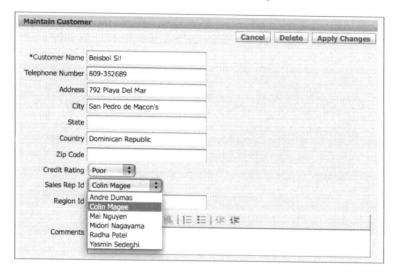

We may also want to change the label in front of the drop-down list because we are still asking for an ID, but the user selects a name. We can change this in the item **P5_SALES_REP_ID**. The user will only see the name of the sales representative, but we will save the sales representative's ID in the database. This creates a more usable application for us.

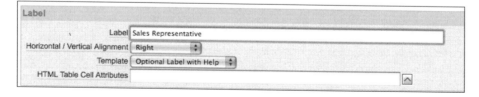

Of course, we can follow the same steps with other ID fields such as the region ID in this particular form in the newly-generated application. Once we have created an LOV in our application, we can also use it in different forms in the application. In the **S_ORD** form, we also encounter the sales representative's ID Item. Just change the value of the displayed section as a **Select List**, change the display name, and set the value of the named LOV. We will get the form that looks like the following screenshot:

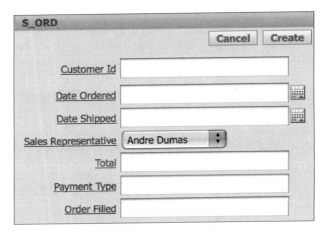

Validations

To help a user understand the business rules that are in the application, we want to have some clear validation messages. In Oracle Forms we have the **When Validate** triggers that can be very helpful to do this, and in APEX we have something called validations. We have one of these triggers in our **S_ORD** block. It's used to tell the user that the date an order is shipped can never be before the date it's ordered. We will put this validation into our APEX application.

```
Block Trigger Details

         Block Name: S_ORD
Block Trigger Name: WHEN-VALIDATE-RECORD

Trigger Text:

IF :S_ORD.date_shipped < :S_ORD.date_ordered THEN
   MESSAGE('Ship date is before order date!');
   RAISE FORM_TRIGGER_FAILURE;
END IF;
```

When we take a look inside page 7 in our generated APEX application, we see that there already are some validations in place.

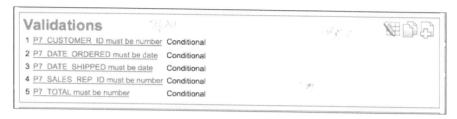

All these standard **Validations** that are in place are defined by APEX itself in order to validate the data that's entered in the specific item. These validations are defined by examining the data types that are in the tables or views that the page is built on.

Now, we will define our own validation on the **P7_DATE_SHIPPED** item. We learned from the **WHEN_VALIDATE_RECORD** trigger in the Forms Converter's **S_ORD** Block that when the shipping date is before the order date, we need to raise an error message telling us that it's wrong. To create a new validation, we click on the plus icon in the **Validations** section in the Application Builder. This takes us to the next page.

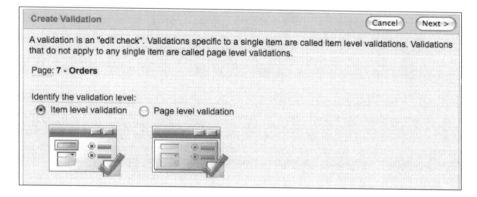

In this first page in the **Create Validation** wizard, we need to define on what level we need the validation. In our case, we want the validation only on the **Date Shipped** item, so we select the value of **Item level validation** instead of **Page level**. Click on **Next** to go further and define the validation.

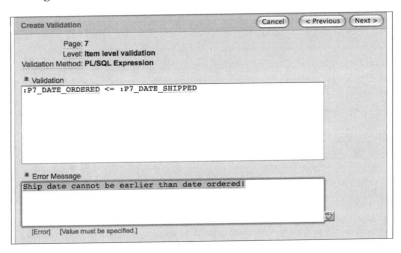

In this page, we can enter the values that define the validation. In the **Validation** field we enter the validation itself, which is the query or summation that defines what we want to check. When the event occurs, APEX gives the user **Error Message**. In our example, we want the user to know that it's not allowed to enter a ship date that occurs before the order date. So we enter the text we want in the **Error Message** field.

Now, we can check if the validation works the way we want it to. Click on the **Run** button on page 7 and fill in the values in an order. Make sure you enter a ship date that occurs before the date ordered and click on **Apply Changes**. We see the error message we entered in two places—on top of the screen in the error box and on the left of the field that contains the **Date Shipped**.

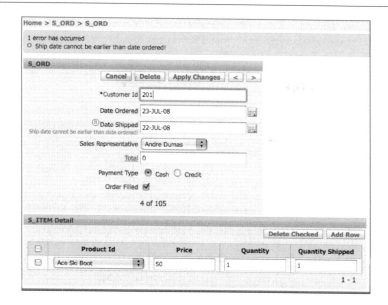

Back to the project page

We already discussed that the project page in our Conversion project is always leading. Now that we have done some work on the APEX application, we want to track the changes we made in the project page. To edit the progress in here, we need to go to the elements in the conversion project and complete them.

For example, take a look at **Annotations** in the WHEN_VALIDATE_RECORD trigger for which we just created an APEX validation in the **Date Shipped** item on page 7. We navigate to the triggers in the Orders Forms application on the project page and select the trigger in question. Let's take a look at the **Annotations** section.

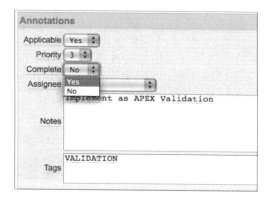

We have implemented the trigger in the APEX application, and now we can alter the value of the **Complete** field. Set it to **Yes** and we will see that the completion of our project has proceeded. In the same way, we can go through all the applicable elements in our project that have not yet been completed.

Titles and names

One of the easiest ways to edit the look and feel of an application is to edit the names and titles in the application. This gives the user a better understanding of the functionality in an application, and we can better tell how the system works.

When we look at the title on top of our application, we notice that it still has the same name we gave it when we created it. And let's face it, nobody would like to work with an application that's called **FormsConversion1**, would they?

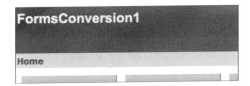

To change the title of an application, we need to navigate to the shared components page in the **Application Builder**. In the shared components, we go to the **Application Definition**.

In the **Application Definition** screen, we go to the **Logo** section. Here we can alter the logo or name of the application. We have the possibility to enter a link to an image that can function as a logo for our application. But in this example, we just give the application a functional name; in my case **Order Management Module**. Click on **Apply Changes** to confirm the new title for our application.

Now, when we run the application, we can see the changes that we made to it. Now we have a correct and functional title for our newly generated APEX application.

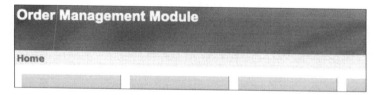

We can do the same to titles of pages, regions, and even labels of items. In this way, we can create a fully functional and logical application.

Summary

In this chapter, we saw a few ways in which we can alter and customize the application we generated using the Forms Converter in APEX. There are some crucial parts that we need to get into our application ourselves. There are also the following user interface tweaks that we can perform in order to create a useful and functional application:

- We can alter the menu on the home page in the generated application by editing the names and images on the **List Entries** that define the menu
- We can create functional **Lists of Values** in the shared components of the application we generated
- The Lists of Values can be used throughout the application
- Functional validations that come from the **WHEN_VALIDATE** type triggers in the Forms Application can be used in the generated application by using the Validations in APEX
- We can track the progress of our conversion project in the project page by editing what we changed so far
- The simplest way to improve the functionality of an application is to change the names and titles of pages, items, regions, and the application itself

8
Delivering your Application

We have successfully converted our Oracle Forms, Reports, Menus, and Libraries into a working APEX application and now we need to deliver these to the users. This means that we have to take a few necessary steps, including the communication with user groups. Because of the simple build options of APEX, we are able to deploy the application we created in a simple and constructed way. Also, there is the possibility to combine applications and integrate them with each other and with the existing authorization schemes.

In this chapter we will learn some things we need to do in order to successfully deliver the application to people who will actually work with it.

Steps in application delivery

In the entire process of Forms to APEX conversion, we differentiate three different phases. We are now in the final stage of delivering the application.

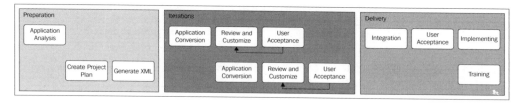

In the **Delivery** stage, there are four parts to be distinguished. They include **Integration** of all the modules and iterations, the ever-so-important **User Acceptance** test, **Implementing** the application on the production environments, and **Training** the users in the new functionality of their beloved application.

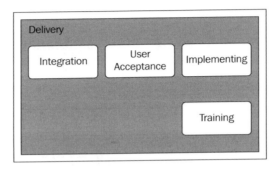

All four steps are important for the success of the application. When we deploy a working APEX application that has just been converted from Oracle Forms, we have the responsibility of delivering it correctly. When we complete all the four steps in delivering the application, we make sure that the users get a functional and working application in their hands.

Integrating modules and applications

For simplicity reasons, we will call every application we created in APEX using the Forms Converter, a new module in this chapter. In the tutorials of this book, we created only one module, so you might want to read through it. But if you are developing and converting a bit more than just one Oracle Forms application, this part is very important. Now it's time to combine all these modules together and integrate them with each other.

The modules we created might be combined with each other using a Forms Menu. In that case, we are able to do a conversion of this particular Forms Menu in order to create a new menu application that points to the appropriate applications in APEX. Unfortunately, we don't have this option in our example. So we will create a whole new application that will function as a menu that points towards the applications we created.

First, we will create a new application in APEX from scratch. The reason behind creating a new menu as a complete and separate application is simple; we want the application to be as lean as possible in order to add more modules and applications to it at a later stage.

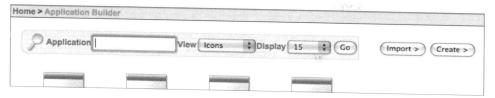

During creation of the new menu application in APEX, we give the application a logical name and set the application ID in such a way that we will not encounter illogical IDs in the future.

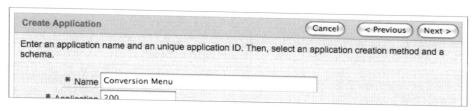

Because we need to create at least one page in every application in APEX during creation, we choose to add a blank page to our application. We immediately name the **Menu**, so there can't be any confusion about its functionality.

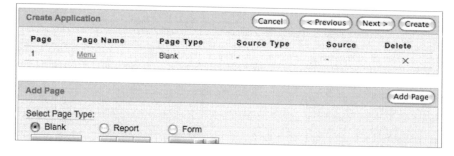

After completely creating the menu application, we will enter all the necessary information. We probably want a menu application that works and looks the same way as the menu in the application we converted, so we develop it in exactly the same way as Forms Converter would. In the new APEX application, we navigate to the **Shared Components** area.

In the **Navigation** section of the **Shared Components**, we find an entry called **Lists**. Go there and create a new list in the now empty **Lists** repository. We are going to create a new list based on a horizontal list with images. To do so, select this option in the **List** template field. Give the new list an appropriate name.

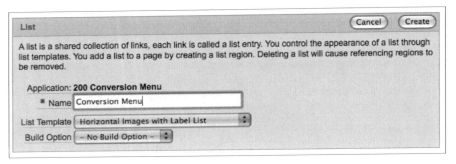

When we have created the list, we can put new entries in it. The list is currently empty, so we can start from scratch. Click on the **Create** button and start with our first application.

In the **Entry** section, we select an image that's appropriate with the corresponding application, and in the **Label** field, we set the name for the application. In our example, we choose an icon that represents a country, some charts, and a few users. The name we give the application is **Orders**.

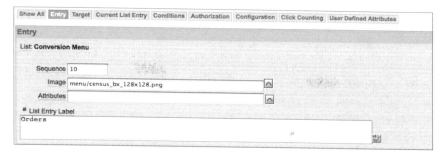

In the **Target** section we create a link to the application we created. In the **Target type** area, we select **URL** as we want the target to be a URL. We can't choose the option to point towards a page in our application because we're not in the same application as the one we converted. The URL we enter is **f?p=102:1**, which means that we want the icon to take us to the application with application ID 102 and to page 1 of that application.

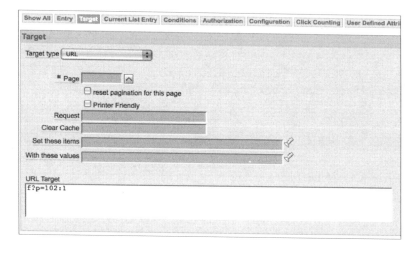

It would be more elegant to enter the target URL in the application as a variable. This means we would need to create an **Application Alias** and a **Page Alias** in our APEX application. In that way, we won't have the target URL hardcoded in the application; but as a simply editable variable. Because when we deploy the application to a different environment (for example, the test or the production database), the application IDs might change. But in our example, we are not likely to encounter this problem, so we just keep it the way it is just now. We will be making sure that the IDs are kept the same over all our environments. But when we're working with the advanced features of **Application** and **Page Aliases**, we will make sure that this goes well.

Now it's time to implement the list we created on **Page 1** in the **Menu** application. To do so, we need to create a new region on **Page 1**. In the wizard that takes us through the region creation, we first select the option that we want to create a **List** region.

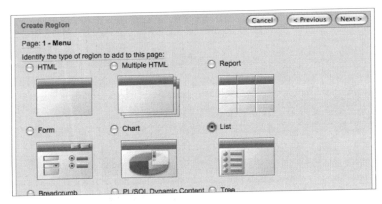

We created the list in the **Shared Components**. This means that we can select the list in the wizard's next page. We called the list **Conversion Menu** and select it as shown here:

When we created the application, we added a blank page that became **Page 1**. This page still contains the blank HTML region in it that was built during creation. Because we don't need that region anymore, we can delete it in the **Page Definition** page.

When we run the application, we see something like the following screenshot. I added a few more links and icons to the list just to show how it would look when we add more converted, or built, APEX applications in the **Menu** application.

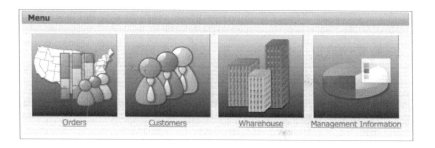

This is the page that the users will see when they log in to the system. The images will take them to the appropriate applications in APEX.

Authentication integration

To have a fully working and functional application, one of the key elements is integration with the existing authentication schemes. In this way, the users can work directly with their new application without having to go through a complete authorization process.

When we want the new APEX applications integrated with the existing authentication schemes, we might want to consider using this. Most Oracle Forms applications use the **DATABASE** authentication and, therefore, we can select this authentication scheme in the APEX application we created.

APEX already has this type of authentication integrated in its systems. In the **Authentication Schemes** part of the **Shared Components**, select the **DATABASE ACCOUNT** authentication scheme so we can use it in our application.

Integrating with Oracle Single Sign-On

One of the advanced features in the **Oracle Application Server (Oracle iAS)** is the **Single Sign-On (SSO)** ability. SSO is used to make sure that the users only have to sign in once for all the applications they are allowed to work in. If the company for which we converted the application uses it, it's a nice addition to the APEX application that we will deliver.

To integrate the converted applications with the Oracle SSO server, we need to create a new authentication scheme in the shared components of our converted APEX application.

In the **Security** section of the **Shared Components**, click on the link to **Authentication Schemes**. In the overview, we get options to create a new scheme. In the wizard that will be presented to us, select the **Based on a pre-configured scheme from the gallery** option. This means that we can select from the options that APEX already has for us.

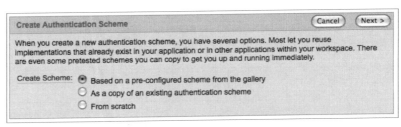

When we click on **Next** in the **Create Authentication Scheme** wizard, we get the overview of the **Gallery** of Authentication Schemes which APEX is able to use out of the box. Select the **Oracle Application Server Single Sign-On (Application Express Engine as Partner App)** option.

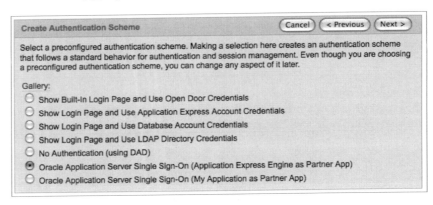

Once we have done this, we can use the SSO capabilities of the Oracle Application Server so the users don't have to authenticate themselves every time they enter an application, now including ours.

User acceptance

Because there are studies dedicated, and entire libraries and dozens of articles written about the subject of user acceptance of software, I will not go too deep into this matter here. But because we have to, I will point out a few things here that will be of importance in a Forms Conversion project during user acceptance tests.

Users must be aware that we create an application that is different from the one they are used to. Because APEX is a completely different tool than Oracle Forms, we will not have the functionality that either we or the users are used to. Test all the iterations and modules in your project separately. The users can get a hang of the new application and issues that always come out just when a user acceptance test is finished. If we start testing after creating all the modules, adjusting them will be harder than when we do it directly after the realization.

When we complete all the iterations, we combine the software we produced to a single, whole application. Now it's time for the users to really use the application as a whole. Some of the aspects that need testing at this point are as follows:

- Does the navigation of the application work? Is it built in such a way that the users understand it?
- Is the look and feel desirable (enough)?
- Are all the validations in place? And are they formulated clearly?
- Do the buttons, links, tabs, breadcrumbs, and so on have the right labels and targets?

Besides these functional requirements, we also have to test some of the more basic requirements. In the requirements engineering world, these are often referred to as non-functional requirements.

- Is the performance of the application as desired?
- Is the integration with the existing authorization working?
- Can the users access the system without hassles?

These and more such trivial questions need to be answered during the final user acceptance test.

Training

To make sure all our efforts for conversion are appreciated by the user group and all the users know how to use the application, we decided that it would be wise to create a small course for the users to attend. This can be done in writing, but preferably in a classroom environment. In this way, we can make sure that the users know how the application works and understand all the things that are different from the original Forms application.

We need to bear in mind that there are some things that the users will encounter. They can be as follows:

- The APEX application works differently from the original Forms application.

- This is a web application, so pressing keyboard shortcuts such as *F5* in the application will not be needed as they will no longer work. There are ways to implement these actions using JavaScript such as the jQuery Hotkeys plugin, which is available on Google Code.

- Navigating through the application will be significantly different. So be sure that the users understand how they need to work with the new navigation and the menus we created. Because the application is running within a web browser, users will automatically try to use functionality within the browser, such as navigating back and forward. Users must be trained not to use these features, or we can deploy the application to our users with the brilliant application from Mozilla called Prism (http://prism.mozilla.com/).

Probably the most efficient way for the users to learn how the new application works is to let them do normal, everyday tasks with the new application. This will help users understand the new functionality quickly and more efficiently. Of course, when the user group is not that big, we might consider doing this during the user acceptance test. In that way, we can add new functionality during the course and understand what we need to change so that the users make full use of the application.

Deploying

When we are done with the user acceptance, it's time to deploy the application in the production environment. We now have a fully working and functional application, so we just have to do this last step in order to make sure that the users can now do their work on a highly performing APEX application. Deploying consists of two major steps—exporting the application and importing it in the new environment (common and necessary for every developed APEX application).

Exporting the application

The first thing we need to do is move the data model to the new database on the production environment. Of course, this has to be done only when we are deploying our new application on a different database (or database schema) than the original Forms application. This will certainly not be the case all the time.

The migration of the data model and the data itself can be done in two different ways—using Oracle SQL Developer (or a different database administration tool), or in APEX itself. In our case, we will be doing it the APEX way.

The **Utilities** part of every APEX workspace has some great possibilities to create a functional DDL script, which we can use to implement the database objects in a different environment. In the following **Generate DDL** section, we will click on the option with the same name as its section:

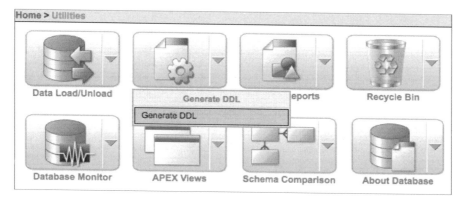

This takes us to the wizard that we use to set all the parameters in order to create the DDL we want. As shown on the following screenshot, on the first page we select the types of database objects we want to create in the DDL. To make it easier for us, APEX has the option to check all the object types. For this, choose the **Check All** option as shown in the following screenshot:

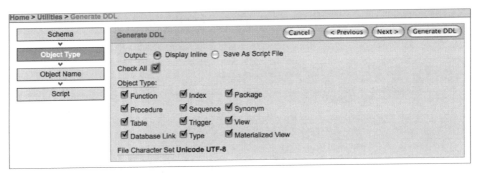

In the next page in the DDL create wizard, we can select the database objects that need to be in our DDL file. In the overview, we are presented with a list of objects where we can select the exact objects and leave everything we don't need. Again, select the **Check All** box and scroll down the list to deselect the stuff we don't need. In our example, this will be the basic database objects in use by the standard DEMO application in every APEX workspace.

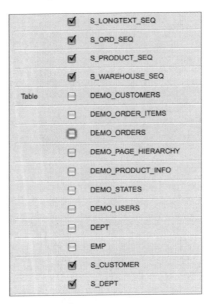

As we have chosen the correct database objects we want in our script, we will go back to the top of the page. Here we have the option to save the DDL script as a script file. We need this option because we want to use it in a different environment.

In the next screen, we get to enter the name we want the script to have and a logical description of the file's purpose.

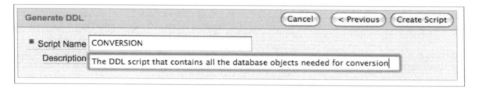

When the file is generated, we will be taken to the **Script** repository as shown here:

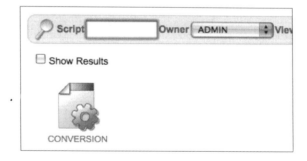

Click on the script icon and review the script. If everything is in place, we click on the **Download** button. This downloads the script for us with the **CONVERSION.sql** name.

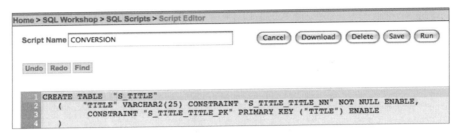

Now we have a full DDL file containing all the database objects we need in our production environment. It's time to make an export of the APEX application we created using the Forms Converter. This is done within APEX itself, as is most of our work.

In the Application Builder, go to the application we created. In my case, this is the application with **Application ID 102**.

As we see in the following screenshot, we have the possibility to export the entire application. To do so, we click on the drop-down box beside the **Export / Import** section, select **Export**, and then click on the **Application** link. This will take us to the **Export Application** page.

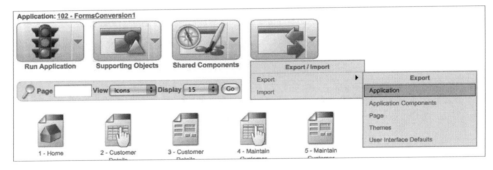

At this point, we need to set parameters for exporting the application to a useful file that we can use to import in the production environment. The information the page asks for creates a file called **f102.sql**. This means we have a SQL file with the number of the application, which is **102** in this example.

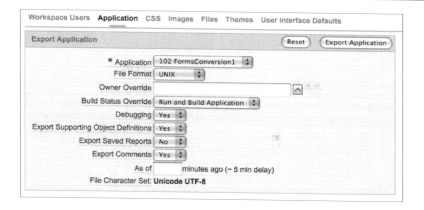

Importing the application

In the workspace on the production environment where we want the application to be implemented, we first need to implement the data model. This is because the application we created needs these database objects in order to be built, and especially to be able to run. Fortunately, we just created a DDL file that does the trick for us.

In Oracle APEX we first go to the SQL Workshop, where we have some options. But to use the DDL script which we created, we go to the SQL Scripts part of the SQL Workshop. To do so, we click on the icon representing **SQL Scripts** as shown in the following screenshot:

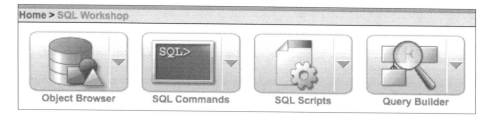

To upload the DDL file we created, we need to click on the **Upload** button on the **SQL Scripts** page in APEX. This action takes us to the **Upload Script** wizard, which is shown in the following screenshot:

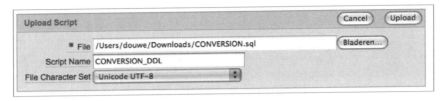

In this page we need to define the script we want to upload to the APEX instance. Browse to the appropriate file and we can optionally give it a different name than what we initially chose. Make sure that **File Character Set** is set correctly. Here we use the **Unicode UTF-8** setting.

When we're done uploading the script, click on the script icon corresponding with the script we just uploaded and see the DDL code.

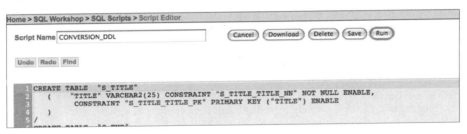

Click on **Run** and this will take us to the following confirmation page:

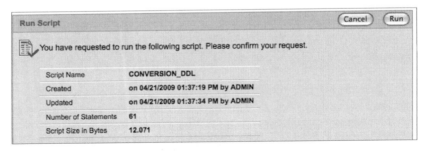

When the script runs, we can look into the results. As we can see, all the database objects in the DDL file have been implemented in the new instance. Because APEX sets the appropriate sequence of implementing the database objects when we create the DDL file, this entire thing works like a charm.

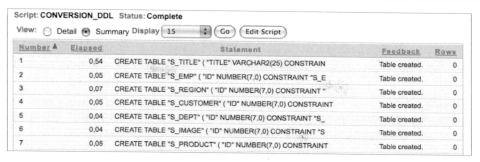

After we have created the workspace in the production database and implemented the data model by running the DDL script we created, we can import the application itself. To do so, we go to the application builder and click on the **Import** button on the top right of the page.

The wizard that will show up takes us to two parts of the import process. First, we need to define and upload the export script we created earlier. This is done by using the following screen:

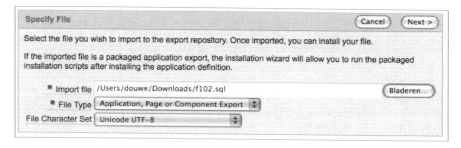

In the **Import File** section, we browse for the **f102.sql** file we created during export. We set **File Type** to its default value **Application, Page or Component Export** and leave the **File Character Set** untouched. By clicking on **Next**, APEX uploads the export script and takes us to the confirmation page that is shown next:

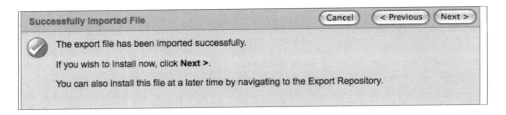

In the next step we need to specify what we want to do with the creation script—on which schema we need to pars it on, do we want to build it or just run it, and what do we want to do with the application ID. In this example we choose to reassign a new application ID

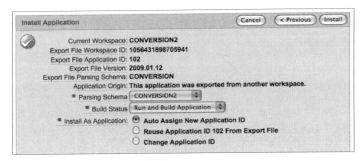

When we click on the **Install** button, APEX will install the application for us. This may take a while and we will see a progress bar in our screen until the application has been installed.

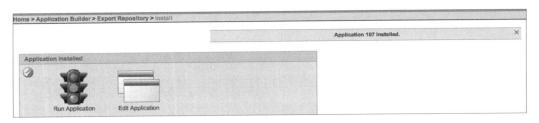

When we come to this page, which confirms that we successfully installed the APEX application in its new workspace, we're done!

Summary

Delivering the APEX application still contains a few crucial steps. But when we have done these steps, we will be done with our Forms Conversion project. Integrating with each other and migrating the converted applications to a new environment marks the take into production for our project.

- When we have converted more than one module to a Forms application, we can integrate the applications with each other using a menu-like application. This application has the same look and feel as the rest of the applications and gives us a single point of entry to the completely converted system.

- We can integrate the new APEX applications into the same authentication scheme used by the Forms application. This gives us the flexibility to reuse the existing users and roles. The integration can be done in various ways, such as database account authentication and also advanced Oracle Single Sing-On integration.

- When we have combined the modules we converted, we can perform an overall user acceptance test. This is done to verify the functional and non-functional requirements of the system.

- Training of users is very important for the success of the implementation of the converted application. Users will not get the same application that they're used to. The best way to perform this training is to do some live actions with the application, letting the users actually work with the new APEX system.

- Deploying the applications to a new environment is done in two major steps—exporting the database objects and the application itself, and importing them into the new APEX environment later.

Index

R

Report Files
  converting, to XML 29
ruleflow. *See* **Drools Flow**
rwconverter command
  about 31
  parameters 31

S

Single Sign-On. *See* **SSO**
Sprint Wireless Toolkit 3.3.2. *See* **SWTK**
SSO
  about 135
  APEX application, integrating with 135

T

tags 79
target database
  about 37
  database objects, exporting 37
  database objects, importing 37
  DLL script, implementing 39
  DLL script, running on APEX 41, 42
  DLL script, running on OMB database
      schema 40
  DLL script, running on SQL Developer 39
  .sql file, creating 38
  .sql file, saving 38
technicality, Forms Conversion project
  about 18
  architecture 19
  components 19
  Forms Builder 20
training, APEX application 138
triggers
  about 65, 90
  block level trigger 66
  examining 66
  form level trigger 66
  item level trigger 66
  post query trigger 91
  set all block triggers completeness and
      applicability option 93
  types 66

U

user acceptance, APEX application 137

V

validations, APEX application
  about 122
  checking 124
  creating 124
  defining 123

W

When Validate triggers 122

X

XML files
  blocks 34
  creating 26
  Forms Module 34
  Menu Modules 35
  Oracle Reports application 36
  orders_fmb.xml file 34
  PL/SQL Libraries 37
  queries 34

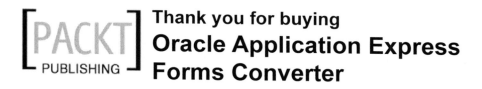

Thank you for buying
Oracle Application Express
Forms Converter

About Packt Publishing

Packt, pronounced 'packed', published its first book "*Mastering phpMyAdmin for Effective MySQL Management*" in April 2004 and subsequently continued to specialize in publishing highly focused books on specific technologies and solutions.

Our books and publications share the experiences of your fellow IT professionals in adapting and customizing today's systems, applications, and frameworks. Our solution based books give you the knowledge and power to customize the software and technologies you're using to get the job done. Packt books are more specific and less general than the IT books you have seen in the past. Our unique business model allows us to bring you more focused information, giving you more of what you need to know, and less of what you don't.

Packt is a modern, yet unique publishing company, which focuses on producing quality, cutting-edge books for communities of developers, administrators, and newbies alike. For more information, please visit our website: www.packtpub.com.

Writing for Packt

We welcome all inquiries from people who are interested in authoring. Book proposals should be sent to author@packtpub.com. If your book idea is still at an early stage and you would like to discuss it first before writing a formal book proposal, contact us; one of our commissioning editors will get in touch with you.

We're not just looking for published authors; if you have strong technical skills but no writing experience, our experienced editors can help you develop a writing career, or simply get some additional reward for your expertise.

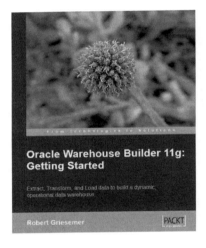

Oracle Warehouse Builder 11g:
Getting Started

Oracle Warehouse Builder 11g: Getting Started

ISBN: 978-1-847195-74-6   Paperback: 330 pages

Extract, Transform, and Load data to build a
dynamic, operational data warehouse

1. Build a working data warehouse from scratch
    with Oracle Warehouse Builder.

2. Cover techniques in Extracting, Transforming,
    and Loading data into your data warehouse.

3. Learn about the design of a data warehouse
    by using a multi-dimensional design with an
    underlying relational star schema.

Oracle VM Manager 2.1.2

Oracle VM Manager 2.1.2

ISBN: 978-1-847197-12-2   Paperback: 244 pages

Manage a Flexible and Elastic Data Center with
Oracle VM Manager

1. Learn quickly to install Oracle VM Manager
    and Oracle VM Servers

2. Learn to manage your Virtual Data Center
    using Oracle VM Manager

3. Import VMs from the Web, template,
    repositories, and other VM formats such as
    VMware

4. Learn powerful Xen Hypervisor utilities such
    as xm, xentop, and virsh

Oracle Essbase 9 Implementation Guide

ISBN:978-1-847196-86-6   Paperback: 444 pages

Develop high-performance multidimensional analytic OLAP solutions with Oracle Essbase

1. Build multidimensional Essbase database cubes and develop analytical Essbase applications

2. Step-by-step instructions with expert tips from installation to implementation

3. Can be used to learn any version of Essbase starting from 4.x to 11.x

4. For beginners as well as experienced professionals; no Essbase experience required

Oracle SOA Suite Developer's Guide

ISBN: 978-1-847193-55-1   Paperback: 652 pages

Design and build Service-Oriented Architecture Solutions with the Oracle SOA Suite 10gR3

1. A hands-on guide to using and applying the Oracle SOA Suite in the delivery of real-world SOA applications.

2. Detailed coverage of the Oracle Service Bus, BPEL Process Manager, Web Service Manager, Rules, Human Workflow, and Business Activity Monitoring.

3. Master the best way to combine / use each of these different components in the implementation of a SOA solution.

Please check **www.PacktPub.com** for information on our titles

2931209

Made in the USA